T0154911

Griefland

Griefland

AN INTIMATE PORTRAIT OF LOVE, LOSS, AND UNLIKELY FRIENDSHIP

ARMEN BACON AND NANCY MILLER

TAYLOR TRADE PUBLISHING
Lanham • Boulder • New York • London

Published by Taylor Trade Publishing
An imprint of The Rowman & Littlefield Publishing Group, Inc.
4501 Forbes Boulevard, Suite 200, Lanham, Maryland 20706
www.rowman.com

Unit A, Whitacre Mews, 26-34 Stannary Street, London SE11 4AB

Distributed by NATIONAL BOOK NETWORK

Photo on page I by Gina Taro Photography

Text design: Sheryl Kober
Project Editor: Kristen Mellitt
Layout: Mary

British Library Cataloguing in Publication Information Available

Library of Congress Cataloging-in-Publication Data

  Griefland : an intimate portrait of love, loss, and unlikely friendship /
Armen Bacon and Nancy Miller.
     p.cm.
  1. Loss (Psychology) 2. Grief. 3. Friendship. 4. Sharing. I. Miller, Nancy. II. Title.
BF575.D35B33 2013
152.4—dc23

                                                                2012017857

ISBN: 978-0-7627-8814-9 (pbk. : alk. paper)
ISBN: 978-0-7627-8972-6 (electronic)

♾™ The paper used in this publication meets the minimum requirements of
American National Standard for Information Sciences—Permanence of Paper for
Printed Library Materials, ANSI/NISO Z39.48-1992.

Printed in the United States of America

This book is lovingly dedicated to Alex Ian Bacon and Rachel Joanne Weiner.

Perhaps starting a new chapter is not so hard, perhaps we are already on our journey.

—ALEX IAN BACON
SEPTEMBER 20, 1981–JULY 17, 2004

The magical child who lives deep inside of me is worthy, honest, and beautiful.

—RACHEL JOANNE WEINER
JANUARY 3, 1988–DECEMBER 25, 2008

Contents

Introduction:
Dancing in the Dark

HELLO, DEAR READER.

We never imagined ourselves writing this book. In a freeze-frame, life-altering moment, we found each other in desolate, uncharted territory, surrounded by chaos and uncertainty. Our two youngest children were dead—Armen's son, Alex, and Nancy's daughter, Rachel. One of our children died in the heat of a summer's day. Another perished on a wintry Christmas night. Without hesitation, relying solely on intuition and an instinct for survival, we locked arms and ventured upon a death-defying excursion, one that would change us forever—from the inside out.

If you are perusing these pages, you too must be here for a reason. Maybe you are picking up this book because you are looking for comfort, answers, something to stave off the terror of having lost your son or daughter. Maybe you are close to someone who has lost a child or loved one, and not sure what to do or say.

Like you, we found ourselves knocked to the ground by death, groping in the dark, yearning for some voice that could provide a shred of hope to remind us we would smile again, feel anything besides dismembered and frayed. But in the startle of disbelief, we had to decide how to live life in this new condition, one that now required us to make choices about our own afterlives.

How true the adage that you get to know someone best when traveling together. As we unraveled our life stories, we discovered an unbreakable bond while traversing the terrain of grief. Armen's history was easy reading, in nice, neat order, while Nancy's was riddled with obstacles and extenuating circumstances.

Armen was born and raised in California. It was her childhood mecca, neighborhoods drenched with cousins, eccentric aunts, uncles, and friends. Her mother adored her three daughters and was the family's center of gravity. Her father was an ambitious and brilliant man, rarely showing affection but always supporting his children's hopes and dreams.

In return the girls succeeded in school, careers, and family life. Her father walked Armen down the aisle, welcomed her new husband, and was present for the birth of his first grandchild, Danielle. Sadly, he died weeks after Alex had been conceived, never living to meet his first grandson.

Nancy was the child on whose survival all hopes were pinned. Her mother's first two pregnancies had ended in stillbirths. Later on, her erratic mood swings and rage fits were unnerving, violent, and always directed toward her daughter. Nancy left home abruptly at age seventeen, realizing she was not living in a safe place. The decision was applauded by loving relatives and friends who had nurtured her through childhood in an effort to provide a sense of normalcy.

Throughout this grief journey, we've leaned on each other's shoulders, borrowed makeup to cover tearstains, and stayed up into the wee hours rehashing our children's lives. Through this unlikely pact born of tragedy, we have discovered the medicinal power of friendship.

From afar you will note striking differences between us. Armen's petite frame and wild brunette mane are surefire signs that she possesses a gypsy spirit, attributing her love for travel to being an identical twin, an embryo split in two, always yearning for the missing part. She travels light, taking bare essentials only (as long as you don't factor in jewelry and shoes). Her passport is always current, and occasional airplane turbulence doesn't shake her. In fact, Armen can land in Paris, discover that her luggage was sent to Tunisia, and remain lighthearted.

Nancy saw right through Armen's capable "can-do" front from the start, sensing she bore a grave wound, a burden of guilt, something the two women share.

Although Armen presents herself on these pages with fluency, miles of travel, and a long history of wanderlust, she gradually reveals her sense of entrapment and suffocation within the borders of the inescapable place she calls Griefland. It's a place where she has resided for years, ever since she lost her son, Alex.

Before that, life had been so sweet, so uninterrupted by troubles. The children were healthy and vivacious, surrounded by doting grandparents and a circle of community that guarded their well-being. Alex's birth completed the family dream—one daughter, one son, two parents madly in love.

But now not even a more-than-thirty-year marriage, budding life in the form of grandchildren, and the tugs from her strong, tightly knit ethnic family can loosen the grip of her grief.

Nancy is a striking strawberry blonde whose baggage bulges with childhood nightmares and demons. Armen is quick to notice them as they bleed onto the margins of her travel journals. After a turbulent divorce, she retreated from the world in an effort to pick up the shattered pieces of herself.

Nancy had emerged from a marital war zone only barely intact emotionally, but she was lucky enough to find love again and remarry eleven years later. Finally serene and engaging with life again, she was devastated when she, too, lost her child, a daughter. Although her life began to unravel once more, she has demonstrated an indomitable spirit and a passion for discovering this new language she calls grief talk.

If you have embarked upon a similar journey, we encourage you to power down, log off, remember to breathe, and allow yourself to lean on others for as long as you need to. Both your internal and external worlds have endured an enormous blow. From the seasons of the year and relationships with loved ones, to physical side effects and reactions, the impact of this emotional collision is unlike anything else you have experienced. Resist the temptation to hasten your reentry.

One of Armen's friends reminded us that, "As soon as you throw in the first load of laundry, the world will think you are healed."

Like us, you will discover your own survival strategies, and as you do, we hope you will share them with us. Should you have anything you would like to see added, or any other questions or comments about the book, please contact us. Most important, we hope this book gives you the courage you need to embrace life again.

Know that each time you turn a page, we are standing beside you, giving you permission to grieve in any way you need; after all, any way you get through this is heroic. Healing is not a destination, but a lifelong quest. Allow it to beckon you, as it did us. We wish you safe travels. One day, one step at a time.

—Armen and Nancy

Armen Remembers Alex

As I sip my first coffee of the day, I catch a glimpse of the sea of papers scattered across the dining room table. This has become home, a resting place now, to the hundreds of journal entries and unfinished sentences describing my recent travels. Off to one corner are hundreds, maybe thousands of e-mails collected and printed as mementos, all neatly arranged and paper-clipped together in some sacred order, it seems. My first passport, now a treasured keepsake, lies on top, holding the stories together, firmly, with an almost parental watch, as if awaiting my safe return.

Bruised and battered, this pair of invisible wings has transported me long distances—to exotic destinations, third-world countries, and places whose names I could barely pronounce. Today it sits on the mountaintop of yet another journey, guarding notes jotted in limbo, between the borders of my former self and a new life. Nowhere in sight is there evidence of luggage.

Alex, my son, inherited his love of travel, and especially flying, from me. His dazzling collection of capes filled a child's make-believe costume trunk, conveniently transformed from a mother's hope chest. His favorite, a rainbow of remnant scraps sewn by his grandmother, draped his shoulders every day as an appendage. Mesmerized classmates delighted in watching him twirl until vertigo set in, and he dropped to the ground in hysterics and laughter. His teacher Blanche marveled at the makeshift wings and named Alex *the boy who wanted to fly*.

He also loved flying insects, bugs, spiders—brown, black, hairy, long-legged. While neighborhood children stood three feet back from the creatures or attempted to squish them with their shoes, Alex leaned in carefully, extending his index finger, ever so gently making contact. Once, when he was quite young, my husband and I discovered a scorpion crawling above his bed. There we stood, paralyzed, only to watch Alex's eyes dance with pure desire to befriend and investigate the deadly creature.

A year or two later, we rescued a litter of kittens—five slimy felines born in a stack of spider-infested logs stowed on the side of our house. It happened on a night when the rain pounded so hard that I secretly feared the sky was falling.

Alex had been the first to hear the kittens' high-pitched whimpers through the sound effects of the storm. We pulled them to safety, cut their umbilical cords, wrapped them in blankets, and then drove to the nearest drugstore for eye drops and infant formula. He named the runt of the litter Punjetta, concocted from Punjab—his favorite character in the musical *Annie*. The name signified a protector, a magical genie, someone who could charm snakes and be a trusted confidant. Then Alex lined a shoe box with his favorite washcloth and proudly announced to us that he had a roommate. All but one of the kittens survived, even though their mother had abandoned them. Where was she? I often wondered. How could a mother abandon her babies? Had she been frightened by the darkness of the night sky, the thunderous rainstorm, or was she simply fearful of this new litter of responsibility left to her care? Several years later I was lying awake at night, asking the same questions about myself.

On July 17, 2004, we received the phone call every parent dreads most. Alex had died of a drug overdose. With no itinerary of where the aftermath might take me, I began navigating a very different kind of journey, this one more foreign than any I'd taken before. Feeling stranded, hijacked, and suddenly all alone in the world, I wondered how this could be happening to us. While everyone seemed to be at a loss for words, words were the only thing that kept me alive. I began writing like a madwoman, publishing articles and opinion editorials that openly talked about death, grief, loss. In the summer of 2008, a column titled "The Fog Lifts," published in the *Fresno Bee*, described the twisted path of grief, and led to many invitations to share my story out loud. The most frequent question asked was when I would be writing a book about this unthinkable journey. It was a question I could not answer. Something was holding me back.

Nancy Remembers Rachel

ANOTHER NIGHT WHERE I CAN'T STOP THINKING. I MOVE TO the library and peruse the shelves for a book, just something to help focus my mind, get it off the thing it always gravitates to. That's when the title catches my eye, and my lips and fingers go numb. It was her book. I need air. Grabbing the spine, clutching the book to my chest, I stumble outside. The moon is brighter than usual, a white sliver in the blackness. I bend over the thin, square shape pressed against me.

In second grade Rachel's teacher had assigned a book presentation to be given in front of the class, a terrifying experience for a seven-year-old. Rachel had raced up the driveway as soon as the bus dropped her at the corner, flung open the back door, and asked, "What is the oldest book in the whole world?"

I said, "*The Epic of Gilgamesh*, I think. Why?"

She said, "I want to do my book report on it."

She was scheduled to give the report at the end of the week and I had a copy in our library, so we read it together as she conjured up mental images of Enkidu and King Gilgamesh. She began her report by informing the class that she had read a more-than-three-thousand-year-old book and in the enthusiastic process, captivated everyone—in particular her teacher, who gave her an A. Never had I seen anyone's face shine as much as hers the day she ran into the house, waving that report in the air like a beacon. I ran to meet her and scooped her up, swung her around. She wanted to read it to me again, leaning over the kitchen table. I gave her cookies and rapt attention.

It is a few months after I get the news that Rachel has overdosed. She is dead. I have wandered from room to room and landed in the dark of her closet. I am looking at her tennis shoes, the ones that are wide at the toe—to accommodate her bunions—and narrow at the heel. I can't throw them out. I put my nose into them and inhale, deeply, just barely catching a scent of something mildly sweaty, skin-like, musty. I see her pushing her feet into them, walking through each step of the nightmare that was each day for her. Getting lost, getting found, running away, running for her life, running to me. In another box I have saved her eyeglasses. They are thick, like mine. I hold them up and look through them. What did she see? How did she see? Were the demons so clear to her?

Maybe women are hardwired. From the day our children are born, we are solely responsible for their welfare, their happiness, their futures, their lives. After all, we are their mothers. In the past, when I heard of a young person dying of a drug overdose, I would think the parents were to blame. Then in a moment no human being can prepare for, Rachel died of a drug overdose. Surely I must have caused this. Surely I could have prevented it.

I run movies in my mind of our lives up to that precise moment in time, like a witness sitting in a jury box. I am the judge and jury at my own prosecution. I shout questions at myself: Why didn't you intervene sooner? Why didn't you fight harder for her? Take her to some secluded island? Kidnap her and run away to Mexico? Why couldn't you have been a more loving mother? Where were you when she injected heroin into her veins the first time? *Where were you?* And then, breaking out in a sweat, hands shaking, head spinning, I remember it's too late. My daughter is dead.

And the biggest fear of all is letting go of this guilt. If I let go, will she cease to exist in my mind? In my heart? The deep sense of absence is beginning to feel almost comfortable, as though it's always been there, as though it's some kind of familiar companion. Has it become a placeholder for Rachel? Or do I realize that it will never be that, that she is never coming back, and that I will never feel anything in life again except a sadness that runs so deep, all the way to the bone, that it can't be expressed except in long waves of silence—and questions.

We want certainty. The idea that there are no answers to the questions that haunt us, plague us, torture our every waking moment, is intolerable at times. One of the hardest things to accept about death is that there are unanswered questions we must live with forever. We think the knowing will save us, will help ease the intensity of grief, so we keep hoping and looking for it—but even if we had the answer, it wouldn't save us after all. Questions such as: What was her last coherent thought? Did she overdose deliberately? How will I keep going without her? Would I take her back if I could? *Is* her name Rachel? Or *was* her name Rachel? Can these scars ever heal? Did she know she was dying?

When a child dies, it feels like all eyes are on Mother. What did she do wrong? Where *was* she? Sometimes it's all too much to bear alone. Even if at the core of me, I could know I was not to blame, I can't escape that need to be the sacrificial lamb, to take on the sins of my past, of our family, to try to cleanse all our wrongs through some kind of redemption.

I don't know what Rachel's last coherent thought was, or whether she overdosed deliberately or by accident, but what I'm coming to know is that her death is re-creating me.

First Contact

January 13, 2009

Nancy, my name is Armen. We have a friend, Anne, in common. She e-mailed me about the death of your daughter Rachel. I'm wondering if we might meet somewhere. Even though I don't know you, I feel an urge to wrap my arms around you. We can talk about anything you want or sit in silence. I promise we will just be two women coming together in this moment of darkness, a place I've come to call Griefland. I've been living here for four years, so I'll show you around; we can take a quiet walk. Just the two of us . . .

Armen

"What's the use of wond'rin' if the ending will be sad?" These were the lyrics from *Carousel* that played as I drove north from my downtown office, a thunderous rain pounding across my windshield, Mother Nature appearing scorned and the early-morning gridlock bringing traffic to a screeching halt.

I had written Nancy without hesitation, an obscure e-mail sent in the dark of night, knowingly intruding on her need to be still with the white noise of fresh grief. Mine, in its more advanced stage, had taken up residence beneath flesh and bones, the tremors hidden from plain sight. Admittedly, I was waging a private war from within, the mini-explosions constantly threatening to bleed out.

We had agreed to meet, and from that very first e-mail exchange I found myself wanting to embrace her pain, a pain I secretly hoped I could take in and absorb, shake hands with, make peace with once and for all. Mine had somehow been buried with Alex. Locked away in seclusion. I wanted to relive that first year over again. Grieve out loud. I needed breathing space, time to stare at the walls, curl up in a ball, and lie at the foot of his bed without time constraints or interruption.

Life had bombarded my sorrow, stepping over and through it, forcing me to return to a new normal with few if any adjustments to my everyday life. I resumed my role as a professional woman, wife, designated daughter, now also caring for my mother who had fallen gravely ill. A few short months later, my husband's mother died. We planned another funeral and never looked back. This morning I wanted to convince Nancy to take better care of herself, grant her license to be selfish. The laundry and relatives could wait.

I suggested a place near the college, Uncle Harry's, a popular bagelry, warm and inviting, even for the dreaded conversation I knew ours would be. Nancy taught English at the university and, like me, loved to write. I sensed, even in our first communiqué, that she possessed a kind of warrior spirit we would later attribute to our shared bloodlines and deep cultural roots. One gypsy, one warrior. Something felt right from the moment we met. Was it possible that our Middle Eastern ancestors had prepared us for this precise moment in time, their spiritual energy and presence circling the universe and pulling us together?

Gripping the steering wheel, I headed toward the cafe, suddenly overwhelmed by the all-too-familiar sense of loss and emptiness. In a series of uninvited moments, the instant replay of my own child's death stretched out in front of me. Traveling backward in time, I watched his stiffened body being lowered into the ground while our glazed eyes stared off into space, fixated on some faceless horizon. Silenced and standing by my side was my husband, Dan, now forced to make good on his nuptial vows to love me "for better or worse." Even his thriving law practice could not salvage this moment of heartbreak. The verdict, a pair of life sentences, had been delivered.

What must have been going on in our daughter Danielle's mind as we lowered her brother into the ground? Profound sorrow? Anger? Survivor's guilt? She stood next to her new husband, Grant, two newlyweds just beginning their lives together. I wanted to grab both of them, sparing us all from the moment, and flee the tragic scene, but stood frozen in solitude instead. Everyone suddenly disappeared, evaporated. In an indescribable moment, something in me perished.

Alex had been the child with a mind all his own. His creative spirit, an unworldly sensitivity to things around him, and an urge to explore life outside the margins had been his trademarks. By contrast, Danielle had excelled in school, was an accomplished pianist, and was everyone's best friend. By anyone's standards, we were a perfect foursome. Summers at the beach, holidays surrounded by much-loved relatives, and the rich aromas of deep roots and family traditions. Destiny had graced us to live happily ever after.

I had enjoyed my share of thrill rides and adventure. I left home in 1972 to study abroad, making the journey solo, settling in the south of France, a pilgrimage to sort out identity, test personal limits, and escape the parental and cultural boundaries I feared might be stifling me. Six thousand miles from home, I made my first journal entry, noting that nothing could be more life-changing, more infinite with possibilities. This, I believed, would be the journey of a lifetime.

My travels took me to all corners of Europe. Before returning to American soil, I visited the Middle East, befriended young Turks, was robbed and mugged by Italian thieves, and burned my corneas on the shores of Athens. I wrote elaborate letters home describing every detail of my harrowing adventures. But they would only set the stage for something far more daring awaiting me in some distant, invisible future.

Missing my turnoff, I pulled over, took a deep breath, and reoriented myself to the streets I had traveled for most of my life. What was today's date? Where was I? Who was I supposed to be meeting? Although it was early January 2009, that other date, July 17, 2004, was still waiting for me on a blank page, surfacing again in all its horror, stinging through tear ducts and leaving a trail of mascara running down my face.

The surface streets leading toward the college were also flooding, a welcome mat now for the arrival of misplaced and forgotten memories: the day I sensed something was horribly wrong with Alex, finding layers of lies and hidden evidence of his self-destruction, knowing death was imminent, in desperation writing a farewell letter, letting go, wanting my life back.

I had once confessed these words to a therapist, only to hear a voice saying, "This *is* your life."

A few weeks later, in a brief, lucid moment, one of our last as mother and son, we sat under a moonlit sky and discussed writing a book together. It would be a mother and son's perspective on this seemingly endless journey, one we both knew was spiraling to an end.

"What would you want to say, Alex?" I asked.

"I never wanted to hurt you, Mom." He looked out into the darkness, his voice shaking. "Do you know that? I mean, do you really know that?"

"Yeah, I do."

"But I have hurt you. I guess we need to start there."

Now I was quiet, not wanting to see him put even more pressure on himself to conform, to be the perfect son. "We can move on from here, though, honey. What could we tell other families that might be hopeful?"

"Let's write about living every moment as though it's going to be your last one. Let's tell people to hug more, like we do. Can we do that, Mom?" In that moment he was a toddler again, all sins washed away.

As I drove across town to meet Nancy for the first time, I could feel my flesh tightening, a chill running down the back of my spine, an uneasy churning creating knots in my gut, all hinting at the potential significance of this meeting. I was running late. Would I be too late to help Nancy, too? The madness began swirling in my head. I nearly missed the turn into the crowded parking lot, a field of concrete filled with college students all too young to know death on a first-name basis. I wanted to blend in but suddenly felt very out of place, as if I were trying to return to some time frame anchored by bliss and innocence. These days, it was hard to fit in. Life was different now. It had been more than four years since Alex's death, but I was still residing in some parallel universe reserved for the grief-stricken.

His room had remained vacant since the night he didn't return home. I had considered redoing it, transforming it into a writing studio, convincing myself it would be the perfect way to honor his spirit, but I changed my mind at the last minute. There was an eerie temptation to leave things exactly as they were at the time of his departure, as if he might return home at any minute and resume life as our son. The mere thought gave me license to venture into the otherwise darkened room, pillows still fluffed, treasured artifacts still on display, childhood photographs shining through glass, images now of a life interrupted. I knew it was probably time to donate the clothes to charity, but I couldn't.

We buried Alex, and these memories would lie dormant until the morning I met Nancy. The sky appeared dark and ominous. Feeling unprepared, naked, that same stark undressed feeling I had in those first moments after learning my son had died, I felt the urge to run for cover. But instead I walked toward the glass double doors. I knew she would be waiting for me inside. When I gazed across the room, our eyes locked immediately.

Our stories were remarkably alike. Although she was just beginning her grief travels, an instant bond formed between us.

We talked endlessly, using unscripted words that mothers never imagine having to say. She needed to share details—the texture of her daughter's hair, the sound of her voice. Trying to be a good listener, yet mindful of the wave of grief that was beginning to overcome me, I leaned into the table, fiercely attuned to her anguish. We quietly acknowledged our children for bringing us together. In that moment, the idea for this book was born.

Was it humanly possible, we wondered, to travel this road together and use it as a newfound reason for living? Could walking the rugged terrain make us more human, better stewards of life and humankind?

Although we only lived about ten miles apart, we agreed to communicate mostly through e-mailing each other day and night, eventually producing volumes of unabridged thoughts, describing in excruciating detail this life after death. Intimate and uncensored, the volley of e-mails would become the diary of our travels for one entire year. Forging a no-holds-barred kind of friendship, we embarked upon our journey. Grief had split us wide open and nothing would be off limits.

I had wondered if our encounter would be tearful, strained, or a mélange of mixed emotions. It turned out to be all of these things, a soulful connection between two women, each of us navigating an unfathomable journey. As I listened to Nancy's words, my own grief seeped through. This was not residue grief or sympathetic grief; this was a grief buried meticulously and carefully in order to get on with life.

Neither of us sipped coffee or tasted bagels that morning. With our eyes locked, voices slow and deliberate, I remember at some point hearing the sound of rain subsiding, watching the hint of sunlight appear through the reflection of double doors, doors we would eventually open and walk through in tandem.

It would be in the intimacy of this new friendship that our grief would find safe harbor, allowing us to share our deepest secrets, our darkest moments, and even our most outrageous fantasies.

"I wonder what those two rascals are up to," Nancy would one day write, in a midnight e-mail.

"They might be dancing," I would reply.

January 14, 2009

Nancy,

There is so much I want to say this evening—about your loss, about our meeting, about this journey we are both traveling. Until this very moment, I have walked it alone, solo, crashing into walls, walking in circles, uncertain where the path was leading. Tonight I feel less afraid and more certain that it is possible to survive this grief ordeal. Having you by my side has already given me renewed spirit and determination.

Armen

Weathering the Perfect Storm

January 15, 2009

Armen,

It's as though we are so many dots scattered across a page, and we come closer to each other because of death. A child dies, and a whole world is affected. Dots start moving, closer to one another, farther away, then closer together. Then two random dots that have never come together before start moving in their inevitable journey toward some kind of energy they can't understand or explain, and a new force is born . . .

Nancy

Armen was late. Though I had no previous description, I believed I'd know her instantly. Rachel had died three weeks earlier, and as it poured rain outside, I felt the internal storm clouds gathering again. As I held our table, searching each face that passed through the swinging glass doors, an elderly woman approached the table, asking me if I'd found her key; she'd been looking under all the tables for it. Was she crazy? Had she really lost a key? A key to what? Then my mind traveled to another moment, as it often did these days.

We had a small dinner party on Christmas night 2008, the night Rachel died. My best china and silver was laid out across the dark wood table, burgundy, amber, royal blue, and emerald-green wineglasses carefully set to the right of the plates, while napkins folded in the shape of a rose were centered in each. An old friend and former professor of mine sat at the head, my son and I were facing each other, and my husband, Randy, was at the other head. I think we were listening to Frank Sinatra Christmas carols, or it might have been some old jazz. At about ten o'clock I looked at everyone and said, "Something is going on with Rachel." I didn't know what, but I felt she was dropping off to sleep. I have no distinct memory of having said this at the time, but my friend would repeat it later. It struck him as odd and out of context.

Just the week before, on the nineteenth, I had spent my last evening with Rachel. She was out of rehab, relapsing again, and we had agreed that she would not be allowed to come home until she could demonstrate she was clean for at least one year. In the interim I met her in the city she lived in about an hour and a half away, which is where I drove on that last late afternoon. The sun was setting, and we were going to have dinner together. When I saw her, we ran toward each other as always, hugging, kissing, taking each other in. We went to a Mexican restaurant she had wanted to try. Her hair was a halo of ruddy auburn ringlets framing her face.

At some point while we awaited our entrees, she excused herself to use the restroom, but after a full fifteen minutes, I knew she was using one of the stalls to shoot up. Her veins were blown, and she went in through her neck, I would later find out. That must have taken her longer. When she returned to the table, she had a too-mellow look about her eyes, her demeanor had changed, and I recall thinking, *I've lost her.*

Over the next couple of hours, we tried to talk, and I said something I regret. But it came through me more than from me, as though I didn't have any free will anymore, as though it was coming from another faraway place.

"Rachel, I'll be okay." It was as though I not only knew she was going to leave me, but that I was giving her permission, something that must have surprised even her. She looked at me, cocking her head to one side. Then a slow, very slight smile began to form on her full lips. The corners of her eyes narrowed, as though she was trying to see something more clearly, fixed on my own eyes. My heart was lurching in my chest with each syllable. I didn't even know if I was telling the truth. How could I possibly know what the truth was? All I knew was that I needed to let her off the hook. I needed to let her go, to let her know I loved her no matter what, and that she didn't need to compound her grief with guilt.

"Thanks, Mom." The voice was a whisper. Her smile became wistful, but it lingered on her face until nightfall. When it was time for us to part, we grabbed each other in a desperate embrace. That singular embrace is my last memory, pressed permanently into my skin. It was more of a clutching, fingers etching into each other's backs. I inhaled her hair. We were both weeping, neither of us wanting to be the first to break the chain, turn away from what was warm and real into the coldness of the night. Then we stood there for at least ten minutes, the stars closing in an arc around us, a breeze kicking up. Something was different. Even the air hurt.

In the four years prior to her death, signs of Rachel's addiction slapped our family—her father (my former husband), our son Josh, and our oldest daughter Jessica—but we picked up the gauntlet and committed ourselves to helping her. My former husband and I researched rehab facilities that specialized in adolescent drug addiction. We settled on a private residential school out of state. Rachel got off drugs, at least while she was there, and received daily therapeutic intervention. The program included the entire family, so we attended the seminars, had weekly phone conferences with her therapists and caretakers, with her and among ourselves, analyzing every aspect of her disease process, what had caused it, how we could make it go away, how we could change ourselves, her, the world, reality.

Eventually she transitioned home, only to relapse again and again, each time more severe than the last. We became aware of how much control the addiction had over her, and felt more and more as though we were being forced to watch her slowly drown, our feet embedded in cement.

On December 26, 2008, in the early morning, Rachel's father called to tell me she had overdosed the night before, and that she was dead. Although I had heard the ringing since two in the morning, and already knew what I would be told, I chose to ignore it. I couldn't bear to hear the words spoken aloud any earlier. I finally picked up the phone at sunrise.

In those first few days, I couldn't see past anything else. Rachel's death was everywhere I went, in every face I saw, in everything I did. I felt isolated, an alien. My husband was Rachel's stepfather, so even he, the person closest to me, did not feel the same degree of devastation. Josh and Jessica would not speak of her. I knew they were both distraught, but no one was talking. We all seemed hermetically sealed in our own bubbles.

"Nancy?" I looked up and there she was, standing in front of me. Armen. Her curly brown hair was blown around her face, a few strands caught in her eyelashes. She looked harried, wet from the storm. We were quiet at first, eyes locked on eyes, absorbed in taking each other in. We didn't talk about anything I thought we would talk about. I described the texture of Rachel's hair, how it smelled in winter when she had come in from the rain. We talked about Alex's eyes, his lustrous curls, how Armen recently saw a model in a magazine who looked like his double. We fantasized about what he might look like now. We didn't share any history of ourselves, none of that "Where did you go to high school?" stuff. We shot straight through to that place that hovers above the everyday rhythm of life.

I sensed a strength and endurance in her, some power she exuded that was quiet and secure. I felt a sense of safety with her, as though I'd just been thrown a lifeline. There was a silent recognition that the chemistry between us was magnificent, extraordinary. It was just a few weeks after Rachel's death, but we entered into a pact on that stormy day, and something was born. Something that, this time, would not die.

January 16, 2009

Nancy,
How do I know you are the right one for this project? I admire that Rachel was outlandish enough to make her exit

on Christmas Day. The fact that she was a beautiful, brilliant redhead who liked to write also caught my attention. I love the way you describe her. I am taken by the things that matter to you. I know you will tell the truth and walk the extra mile of this journey. Something tells me that what we are about to do may become the most important chapter in our lives.

Armen

Sorry for Your Loss

January 17, 2009

Nancy,

Today I need to talk with you about those first days. I need you to know me, to know what this was like, opening card after card as though I were in some kind of nightmare. Everyone was silenced by Alex's death. As I return to those boxes of first sympathy cards, fixated on the repetition of "there are no words," I cringe at the thought that you are now reading these same hollow phrases that, despite good intention, can't penetrate the numbness. In time people will need to know you are okay, so they can return safely to their own lives, confident that nothing like this could ever happen to them . . .

Armen

In those first days and weeks following Alex's death, my once quiet mailbox was crowded with cards and letters, even books that arrived in large padded manila envelopes, some bulging with Bible verses, promises of healing, watermarked with faint, pastel florals, religious symbols, and the words *with deepest sympathy*. All were intended to offer hope and support, but most only added weight to the nagging hurt, the pain that exploded from my chest, the invisible wound that felt wide open and exposed, so much so that I feared I was bleeding to death.

My husband and I opened cards, one after another, as if the next one might offer a cure for the terminal heartache we were both suffering. The words somehow seemed flimsy, inadequate, redundant. Eyes bloodshot, bodies aching with exhaustion, we had lost sight of the love or compassion with which these notes had been so painstakingly written. Some came from complete strangers.

"Who is this person?" I asked my husband, Dan, repeatedly.

Neither of us was functioning; there was mental confusion, sleep deprivation, and mountains of cards. Deciphering signatures, we paused long enough to nod at someone's thoughtfulness, but even this small cerebral movement was tedious. The flurry of mail sent with good intentions, night after night, for us was dreaded, unwelcome. We were starving for privacy. Time to gather our wits.

Some notes were stuck beneath the welcome mat at the front door, the same spot we'd discovered the coroner's card a few days earlier. The notes were intrusive, as if written by a voyeur peering through the front window, watching us undress our sorrow in the dark. We sifted through more cards; many by now were duplicate images, subdued shades of sadness, varying degrees of apology. Everyone was sorry. And at a loss for words. Like us, no one was prepared for that moment.

Mere words, however heartfelt, cannot provide even the slightest balm to ease the hurt.

The anguish you are feeling has to be beyond description.

Words are so insufficient, but they are all we have.

The cards became a daily reminder that someone in our family had died. Occasionally I would find a different kind of note that reminded me to stop and think for a minute about the broken parts, those pieces inside that nobody could see, the pieces that were shattered, permanently damaged, and unfixable. I held tight to this card. It went into a special pile. It was from someone who had traveled this journey, a woman whose husband died in his sleep. Death was so sudden for her, for us, catching everyone off guard. I remember her telling me she didn't know what to say to her six-year-old. It was the middle of the night. There was so little time to prepare. Never enough time.

My husband would leave the room momentarily, maybe to catch his breath, but would return quickly. Opening mail now required a partner. I couldn't do it alone. We would resume the ritual, opening more cards, trying to stack them neatly, keeping envelopes for addresses. The pile kept falling over. Grief is messy.

The words just won't come.

I have no words.

It's difficult to know what to say at a time like this.

I needed something more—an explanation, words to chronicle this experience, this passage that felt as if it might also take me to the grave. But there were more cards to read. I reached for the next batch of envelopes.

We received hundreds of notes—sympathy cards and letters, ranging from *sorry for your loss, with sincere regrets,* to those extending a hand, the *if there's anything we can do* variety. They came in droves, many accompanied by floral arrangements, incense-filled candles, and ceramic angels. Some of the notes were from strangers who had become acquainted with Alex through his obituary, drawn, I imagine, to his youthful photo, curious about the cause of death, and finally needing to share a bit of the pain as if to acknowledge that society or modern medicine or even the family had failed him.

One of my friends wrote, *Children are a gift we receive on terms we aren't allowed to negotiate. Accepting those terms is our gift to them for however much time we are allowed to have together.* This note went into the short pile, one I still go back to every now and then.

I once read that planning a funeral is like planning a wedding, only you have to do it in less than seventy-two hours. I began gathering photos—all of my favorites—Alex at the pumpkin patch, Alex with his sister, Alex and his cousin Lauren, Alex in the famous Superman cape. Without even a pause, it was time to start writing his obituary. How do you summarize your child's life in column inches? As a writer, I should have known how to do this, but I obsessed over each word, and before I could finish a first draft, visitors and more cards began arriving. The funeral procession was about to begin.

Tragedy is a horrible thing to waste. Many squander it by growing sorry for themselves, drowning their grief in guilt, torturing themselves with endless what-ifs, or growing bitter and angry. As the cards and letters ceased, as people moved on with their lives, expecting us to do the same, we arrived at our own moment of truth. Could we survive this?

The passage of time has been cruel and relentless. Seasons have come and gone, one after another, year after year, all with little mention of Alex, not even at the dinner table during major holidays.

When Nancy and I met, we agreed to document the journey word by word. Hands trembling, we began by constructing simple sentences. Grief is exhausting. Grief sears like third-degree burns. Grief is inconvenient. Memories arrived, uninvited, much like the people who showed up at our front doors to pay their respects. Some of our words were ugly and unsavory, with their own disturbing set of sound effects. We whispered, whimpered, then wailed without the slightest forewarning. Sounds and shrills that no one dared make in public, in church, or at the cemetery. But this was all we had. This new vocabulary, this grief talk, offered hope, a form of oxygen to counteract the despair, keeping us alive at least until the following day—when the sorrow would take hold of us all over again.

January 17, 2009

Armen,

Most people say in their letters, "I cannot imagine what this must be like." Everyone seems to lack language to describe this moment. And what's really ironic is that we ourselves can't imagine this is happening to us. We are just as horrified as each of them.

Nancy

January 17, 2009

Nancy,

And yet we go through the motions of organizing funerals and memorials, returning to work, meeting our cousins for cocktails, inviting family over for dinner, nurturing our loved ones, and then sharing our demise in the privacy of these e-mails. Maybe our husbands see through us, but the rest of the world only sees strong, "exemplary mourners."

"How is she doing?" someone might ask.

"She's really holding up well."

Armen

The Boy Who Wanted to Fly

January 20, 2009

Nancy,

Tonight I walked into Alex's room. It still smells like a teen-age boy, kind of sweaty, musty. Am missing him like crazy. Do you think our kids ever knew how much we loved them? How important their lives were? Tonight I needed a mother-son talk. I wanted to tell him I found a perfect writing part-ner. He would have connected with you. He would have loved engaging in intellectual debates with you, Nancy. You would have marveled at his powers of persuasion.

Tonight I simply asked him to give me the guts to tell this story . . .

Armen

We lived in three houses during Alex's brief lifetime. There was the house where he was conceived, another where he was born, and the third where he spent a majority of his teenage years negotiating with monsters he insisted were hiding underneath his bed. Although I never actually saw them, I could sometimes hear whispers late at night. By the look in his eyes, they were a constant presence hovering around him. Without any warning, he would run like a track star down our two flights of stairs and then stand perfectly still in the middle of the living room with his lanky arms tightly wrapped around himself, his appearance cold and stiff, as if he had just escaped a blizzard or avalanche. His body language, those arms encircling his torso, hinted that my son was holding on for dear life.

As for me, I wasn't doing much better. I feared for his life. A mother knows. When we made eye contact, I could see that he was trying to tell me something but couldn't get the words out, as if maybe he were being held hostage over some important piece of information that only he knew. Without embarrassing him or force-feeding a conversation, I would deliver a dish of his favorite tapioca pudding or hand him a stack of folded laundry and then sit on the corner of his bed to create a moment of opportunity between us. Neither of us was comfortable with the language we were attempting to speak.

By the time he hit high school, his hazel eyes were starting to glaze, diminished in size and clarity. A distant look in his stare gave him the appearance of a stranger or alien, a foreigner, someone I wasn't sure I knew or even trusted. Instinctively, though, I would grab him, as only a mother can when she feels her child is in danger or harm's way, embracing him with a gigantic bear hug, holding on tight until one of us finally let go. On my way out the door I would always remind him, "I love you, Alex."

"I love you more, Mom," he would add, and then quickly shut the door. He always had the last word.

He was a beautiful and spirited child. He loved school, sea creatures, stray dogs, and all things made from sugar. I can still hear the kitchen chair dragging across the floor as he made his way to my mixer, holding out his hand for a sampling of cookie dough or buttercream frosting—anything made from a batter. He was my Cool Whip kid and my favorite sous chef. When nobody was looking he would stick his fingers into the sugar bowl or grab a handful of chocolate chips or miniature marshmallows, stuffing them into his mouth. Years later a friend of mine suggested that sugar was his first addiction.

By sixth grade he was a well-seasoned gifted and talented student, singled out by many of his teachers as someone to watch. One of his teachers pulled me aside during open house to explain that Alex was filled with "insatiable curiosity," a quality he warned could take him to the moon or hurl him over a cliff. "Inquisitive children are always in danger of testing their own limits," he said.

His prized collection of miniature figurines, made from soft, pliable pewter, lived in a secret hiding place in the vicinity of his allowance stash and a pile of cherished sand dollars, collected from our annual trips to the beach. He would spend hours choreographing them into formation while I did household chores one floor below. I could hear him voicing each of the characters and interrupting them with explosive sound effects, the kind generated by a little boy's imagination. When he tired of them, he would move to the plastic bin of art supplies that was kept in his closet, and using mixed media of crayons and pencils, Magic Markers and paint, he would create Alex Art. That's what we called it. His elaborate sketches resembled Escher drawings, embellished with lizards, prehistoric figures, and—now that I think about it—too many dark colors. Once he told me he was drawing his dreams. Days later I would discover the drawings crumpled up and discarded in the trash or shoved underneath his mattress.

We began noticing subtle changes when Alex entered his teens—a hush or secrecy that seemed a bit abrupt, but then again, adolescence is an awkward passage even for the brave of heart. Comparing notes with friends, I was reminded that it was a natural time to start distancing yourself from parents. Alex and I were especially close, so this didn't quite fit, but I was starting to feel like a stereotypical ethnic mother holding on to her son in an obsessive, clingy manner. Reluctantly, I loosened my grip. For a short time it seemed to give us both a bit of breathing space. But then his middle school counselor made an observation that she had seen Alex wandering around the perimeter of the school grounds all alone at recess. Visualizing this crushed me; how could my gregarious little boy suddenly be a loner? Almost overnight his straight A's began melting into C's and D's.

At "back to school night," two of his teachers commented that he was missing classes, not turning in homework, falling asleep on his desk. We confronted him. Conversations turned into inquisitions. Alex, known for his truthful nature, admitted everything. Marijuana. Over-the-counter allergy pills. Cough medicines. Hallucinogens. His childhood fascination with creepy-crawlers had grown daring, sophisticated, life-threatening. He was enchanted by the world of drugs. There were days I would physically walk him to class, stalk him from the parking lot, ensure he was not leaving his classes or campus, but there's only so much policing a mother can do.

My husband refused to be his son's jailer. During the next several years, we would try tough love, Al-Anon, therapy, inpatient rehab, anything and everything. A parent never gives up. Besides, it felt more like a bad dream than reality. I was sure that at some point, we would all wake up and move on with our lives.

By the time he turned eighteen, drugs had become a steady part of his daily regime. He left trails everywhere: tiny foil wrappings, ziplock bags, remnant powder on his countertops, empty prescription bottles. There was paraphernalia, too: tarnished spoons that had been darkened by matches, blown-glass accessories, clips for holding illegal possessions. We were outraged at first, but the repetition of this scene became commonplace in our otherwise pristine home.

At one point I grew so accustomed to finding the paraphernalia that I picked the pieces up as if they were dirty laundry and then escorted them down to the garbage can. I had become numb and silenced by the routine appearances of these items, by the constant denial and excuses offered by my son, so much so that I wondered if I was imagining something that wasn't really happening and simply going mad. Everyone I spoke to seemed to defend Alex, explaining that he was a normal, adolescent boy, experimenting with manhood. Even his pediatrician assured me he was fine. But I knew better.

Then came September 11. I was dressing for work and coaxing Alex from bed to get him off to school when the phone rang and someone told me to turn on the television. In the next moment I was watching an airplane fly into one of the Twin

Towers. The newscasters kept repeating the story over and over. Their voices, I remember, were breaking, something you rarely see among professional journalists.

Alex came downstairs, saw the look of horror and utter disbelief in our eyes, and without a word walked to the refrigerator to grab a Coke and bowl of cereal. He had no reaction. To this day, the expressionless look on his face remains trapped in my memory, replaying with as much intensity as the chilling sight of the Twin Towers collapsing and scattering lives and ashes everywhere. I went to church that day and prayed for the victims of 9/11, but mostly I prayed for Alex. I started believing there was a monster living inside my son.

Even his comic book heroes transformed into creatures who could obliterate the world. He drew them with sharp angles and droplets of blood falling onto the paper. He was obsessed with video games and computers. Friends stopped dropping by. His world became small and dark, confined exclusively to his room between midnight and dawn while most people were sleeping.

Eventually, when the voices of addiction became too disruptive, he would stop what he was doing, walk outside onto the balcony, and stand frozen for hours, grabbing hold of the railings, mesmerized by a familiar backdrop of darkness. I can't help but wonder if he ever caught a glimpse of the stars or the moon. Some nights I would go upstairs, stand quietly next to him, trying to ease his pain, drawing his attention to the moon, and so wanting to shine some light onto his face.

I grew exhausted from worry, collapsing late at night into my bathtub, desperate for relief. Even with the water running full blast I could hear the weight of his footsteps pressing against the floor. He paced back and forth across the room. Almost like clockwork, by the time I was ready to get out of the tub I would hear his balcony door open and slam shut.

Sinking deeper into the water, I would look up and have words with him, tears streaming from my eyes, knowing of course that a layer of ceiling muffled my pleas. There were walls and worlds between us. And monsters. Even now, years later, I second-guess myself, wondering if he ever heard my voice crying out to him. I knew he heard theirs.

His high school counselor called us one day with an urgent request for a family conference. We were about to learn that Alex had confided to a student teacher his desire to jump from his bedroom balcony. His words set off an alarming list of school protocols and emergency procedures, requiring us to check him into a psychiatric hospital for seventy-two long hours of observation. I could feel the ground shaking beneath me. I was losing hold of my son. He was imprisoned in his own monster-infested world, barricading himself in his bedroom, painting the walls a dark shade of navy, dark like the night sky. And then he began to disappear. I woke up one morning, my insides screaming, but by then it was too late. A few weeks later I was sitting on his floor, propped up against his bed, writing the obituary.

His door has remained shut for more than four years. His favorite books are neatly stacked. The figurines stand in formation, and one of his famed reptile drawings is now under glass and hanging on the wall in his bedroom. But there is a disturbing sense of something missing. I sneak in now and then when no one is looking to smell his shirts, fluff his pillows, clench the frame holding Alex in his Superman cape, and curse the monsters, daring them to come out from under the bed and look me in the eye.

January 20, 2009

Armen,

I wish I had had a chance to know Alex. How could this happen? And more important at this point, how in the world are you and I going to carry on without them? The families we nurtured now resemble the aftermath of some horrible battle or combat zone. Will we ever believe in anything again?

Nancy

Rachel Is Dead

SAYING HER NAME

February 3, 2009

Armen,

Do you remember that moment when you first said it out loud? It may have been to your mother, maybe to Dan, but when you first said: Alex is dead. AlexAlexAlexAlexAlexAlex-Alex, until every piece of reality is somehow strung together in a long thread of anguish. There is, finally, a strangeness to saying their names, isn't there? When I say Rachel's name out loud, it feels thick coming off my tongue. It's hot in the back of my throat. It feels sacred. When I say Rachel or you say Alex, doesn't it seem as though we're challenging some long-standing belief about permanence or stability? As though we're provoking the gods . . .

Nancy

It was the early morning following Christmas Day 2008. We had just had guests for Christmas dinner the night before. The table still had the used napkins strewn across it, a vision of the last moment of innocence any of us would have. The news came about 7:00 a.m. In that one initial moment, when the shock had not even set in, I watched each of us retreating into some inner layer of experience, somewhere reserved for the quaking of human souls. Rather than embrace one another, we recoiled to solitary places. My son, Josh, walked outside, hyperventilating, calling his older sister, Jessica, to tell her to get home. I don't have any memory of where my husband, Randy, went. I believe he sat in a chair for hours, but I'm not sure.

I somehow moved from the kitchen to a bedroom and called my dear friend Rosemary. In that one moment I needed to hear her voice. She was a mother, her daughter was also addicted to heroin, and they had almost lost her. She was a nurse practitioner. She would know.

I left her a message: *Call me. It's urgent.* She called about ten minutes later. Randy picked up the phone, pausing before handing it to me. I put it to my ear. I heard her say, "Nancy, it's me. Is everything all right? What is it?"

I said, "Rachel. Rachel." And my voice froze in my head. That moment stretched out in front of me for decades, generations, melding past, present, future all together—in some incredible fusion of time and pain and memory.

I realized the words were still locked in my head. I couldn't envision speaking the phrase *Rachel is dead.* If I said it out loud, the reality of this would spill into the world, become part of the moon, the stars, the thread running across the floor, connecting all of us, connecting every person to some moment of shocking loss. It would be real.

I knew this moment would resonate for Rosemary all the days of her life, would cut her to the bone with terrible intimacy, would bring the reality of her own daughter's mortality into penetrating proximity. I knew in the passage of these words, her own heart would pound in her chest as mine was.

"Rachel . . . is dead." Between saying her name and the last part of the sentence, I took a deep breath, as though I were getting ready to lift something heavy. It seemed the space between the words was stretching beyond the borders of time. Then everything stopped. I could hear Rosemary gasp, then she asked if she could come over. I could feel the words like a needle piercing her vein, injecting hot knowledge into her. No going back—not this time. There we were.

"Can you?"

"I'm on my way." Fifteen minutes later, she called to ask for my address, evidence that she, too, was lost and disoriented in learning of Rachel's death. We would all be lost and disoriented for what feels like eternity.

It is two months later. Rachel exists in photo albums, laughing with friends, posing for the camera, waving, kissing and hugging cousins, sprawled over a couch, stretching like a cat over a chair, hair thrown back over a shoulder, impish eyes wide. She is frozen in time and space. She is a shoe box full of artifacts—photos, letters, glasses, a necklace. When I say *Rachel,* the name is disembodied. It exists separately from her beautiful face, full lips, brown-hazel eyes. Like the famous René Magritte painting of a pipe, *This Is Not a Pipe,* when I say *Rachel,* I see that she is not here—the name is a facsimile of her. To say it, then, is to remind me over and over again that there is a space between the word and the person. A space that stretches to the outermost regions of experience. A space that transcends memory. A space that cannot ever be bridged from the material world. Her name hides somewhere behind an unlocked door, a door no one has entered yet, that no one wants to enter. It's safer not to say it at all. If you say it, you also have to say *Rachel is dead.*

Nobody says Rachel's name anymore. I asked my son, Josh, if he found it difficult to utter his sister's name. He said it was very hard. My daughter Jessica never says the name out loud. I said her sister's name once and she paused and then told me it was weird to hear it spoken. I noticed she had taken to using pronouns lately—*her* or *she,* but never *Rachel.*

My mother never says Rachel's name. She doesn't want to upset me. This is not the real reason, though. She avoids the name because she is afraid of her own death, or she fears that saying the name invites death closer into the family circle. Or she is afraid of naming the absence, of giving death a face, a presence. Saying *Rachel* has a new meaning now. But saying her name is not going to upset me. I am already thinking her name continuously. Like a thick velvet curtain that falls in the background of the mind, she's always there.

I want to hear the sound of her name. When I whisper it to myself, under my breath when I'm alone, I see thick, corkscrew red curls, the flecks of brown and green in her eyes that mean Rachel to me. I see her creamy complexion, her arms around an orange tabby. I close my eyes and see a long row of still-life paintings—a string of images, her name, her smile, her laughter, her skin, her fingers with the chewed-down nails painted purple or green. Her name used to mean life, because when we used it, she was alive; her voice and face were connected to the word.

In the morning when I wake up, I remember Rachel is not here anymore, that raw reality of *gone.* As the hours pass,

I look up and see a photo in a frame and recall that Rachel is the photograph now. I move through the day, the evening, the stars come out, the moon rises and falls, I lie in bed with the last thought of the day being that she will never call me again.

I want to say her name, want to scream it, sing it as loud as I can. I want to shout *RACHEL* until my voice cracks. I want to etch each letter into my mind. I want to do this because saying her name may open that door.

February 3, 2009

Nancy,

As time moves on, you will find Rachel with you even in the silence. I've come to feel over the past few years as though Alex lives on the tip of my tongue, in both daylight and darkness. Don't ever hesitate to say "Rachel," Nancy. Doing so keeps her near you, close by. So you remember that neither she, nor you, can disappear.

Armen

WHAT WAS YOUR DAUGHTER LIKE?

February 5, 2009

Armen,

How will I ever be able to forgive Rachel for choosing death over life? I always had this vision of success for my kids: They would go to a university, be passionate about some career choice, get married, and have children. My vision of what constitutes "success" has now changed. Although her brother and sister graduated from universities, have

careers and significant others, Rachel in fact may have been
the most successful of the three—she had something else . . .
something that can't be obtained from a university . . .

Nancy

"What was your daughter like?" is a question I hear often from people who didn't know Rachel—students, friends, or colleagues. I love answering, because it allows me to bring her back into the present tense again.

What was Rachel like? In that ten-second span between question and answer, her life unfurls in front of me. Wild, uncombed, wavy hair. Only a ponytail would keep it mildly subdued. Her eyes had a glimmer that spoke of both mischief and excitement, exuding a contagious energy. Rachel mesmerized everyone she came into contact with. It wasn't just her beauty—I often observed faces turning again and again in her direction—but her sensitivity to everything and everyone around her, her X-ray vision. Her goofy laugh was infectious, a combination of hiccup and gasp.

She had a playful grin she wore most of the time, as though she had a secret she would willingly give up with very little prodding. A reader, lover of all games. Barbie dolls, paper dolls, any dolls. She loved to wear dresses. A girlie girl. When asked in kindergarten what her favorite color was, she said "periwinkle." None of the kids knew that color, so she described it in detail, how you have to mix lavender with light blue and a bit of pink. The teacher mentioned it during the first open house.

In high school she studied photography. She had a collection of cameras and left me hundreds of photographs, mostly of women. On an Amtrak ride home to see me, she took a picture of an African-American woman sleeping across from her, the look of calm and feel of easy motion. Mouth open. Close-up. She was always trying to get close. To capture serenity. Cheshire Cat smile, dimples.

As she grew into an adolescent, her gigantic brown almond-shaped eyes were a perfect canvas for the eye makeup she loved to wear. In the fashion of an Egyptian queen, she reveled in making elaborate brushstrokes, outlining her lids with layers of black liner and mascara. Red lipstick applied with a heavy hand.

But it was her hair people will remember long after everything else pales with time. At the moment of her birth, the first words came from the nurse standing next to the doctor. "Oh, look at that baby's gorgeous red hair!" This would be a common refrain through infancy, childhood, and adolescence. Rachel's hair was not only a magnificent shade of ruddy cranberry but luxuriously thick and curly, a halo of ringlets falling around her shoulders. It would also be the last of her features described. "The extremely curly red hair measures eight inches in length," states the autopsy report. Even in death, a coroner had taken notice. I wondered if he noted the length of all corpses' hair.

Not many knew she was a mean Scrabble player, having been a voracious reader all her life. From the time I was pregnant, I would read stories to her, convinced that if she heard stories while in the womb, she would acquire a love of reading.

When she was a little girl, I would make up tales of young girls who were confronted with problems and found ways to work them out, reciting them to her at bedtime. She listened intently to every word.

As she grew, she devoured everything from *The Chronicles of Narnia* to the *Wizard of Oz* series and every children's classic I could think of, including *Alice's Adventures in Wonderland*, anything she could get her hands on by Stephen King, and Virginia Woolf's *Mrs. Dalloway*. And she was a writer. Even while in rehab, she produced twenty-page letters to me, sharing in grand detail her demons, her hurts, her hopes.

She saw through to the middle of people, to the symbolism of sacred objects, such as a teddy bear. For Rachel, a teddy bear was not just a teddy bear; it encompassed an era in a person's life, reflected childhood, innocence lost, intimacy, friendship, comfort, loneliness, grief. It was a talisman. She knew that nothing was ever one thing.

When Rachel died, I received a flurry of e-mails from people I didn't know. I discovered in reading some of these that she seemed to be able to give to others what she could not give to herself. One letter described her unwavering loyalty and optimism in helping a troubled friend overcome a huge hurdle. During a time when Rachel herself had huge hurdles to work through, she would subordinate them to ease someone else's pain.

What was Rachel like?

Rachel's addiction was like a tidal wave, constantly rising up in front of her. And she met it as a child would, always saying, "No, you will not take me down." But in the end she was no match for it, though she never gave up trying. During the last five years before her death, Rachel admitted herself repeatedly to rehab programs. She would stay clean for days, weeks, sometimes months. She never made it longer than nine months that I know of.

She always saw people as more alike than different. When she was four years old someone had given her an African-American Barbie, and we'd taken the doll shopping later to find a friend. She found another Barbie, this time a white one with the same dress, and thought since they had matching dresses, they would be the greatest of friends. As we stood at checkout, the cashier said, "Why do you have a black Barbie?" Rachel's face was dumbstruck. She stood, examining one doll, then the other, her brow furrowed, her eyes squinting. She said, "But they have the same dress." That was the first moment she was taught to notice difference, instead of to embrace sameness. She was quiet all the way home, but gripped both dolls in her hands.

She seemed, from the very beginning, not to be of this world at all, but part of some distant constellation, or some gale-force wind blowing through all our lives, and then with the quiet of a candle she blew out altogether.

February 6, 2009

Nancy,
Some people live a lifetime studying the classics, seeking out wisdom, searching for meaning, and never obtain the kind

of power you describe in Rachel. This power was so com-
manding, so intense, that it threatened her very existence.
This explains why we have grieved even while our children
were living. We knew they were no ordinary children. Let's
face it—you wouldn't have wanted her any other way. There
is nothing to forgive, Nancy, only to accept and embrace.

Armen

Down the Rabbit Hole

SIDE EFFECTS

February 10, 2009

Nancy,

Have you felt as if maybe our entire composition is chang-ing with this grief condition? My body hurts in the same way my pupils have felt when I've had them dilated. There is a hypersensitivity to the world around me. Tonight all I want us to do is sit in the dark, all by ourselves. Knowing you are at the other end of the computer monitor is enough to sus-tain me until I grow accustomed to this new vision . . .

Armen

Grief blisters like third-degree burns, trying to form scabs, struggling to heal, ripped off without warning by the sight of his favorite things: scuffed Adidas, an autographed Tony Hawk skateboard, Rice Krispies treats, macaroni and cheese from a box. I see him in all these things now, but he quickly evaporates, setting off a silent alarm that plays full volume inside my head.

Music hurts. I've stopped going to the theater. I can't sit for long, can't enjoy the sound of a single note let alone an orches-tra. I am a stranger in my own skin, crawling in quicksand, searching for handrails to keep me upright and vertical. I am constantly walking into walls, tripping over my own feet, fearful that one of these times, I will fall to the ground and dissolve into the earth.

Grief is exhausting. This isn't sleepy tired. This is the kind of tired I felt at the end of my labor with Alex, that sweaty, throw off the sheets, let the air hit you, relax the breathing rhythm tired, that tired I felt just before I slept for hours and hours. Only then, when I woke up, it was for a really good reason. There was a baby to take care of. Someone to love.

Grief is sneaky. It hides insidiously and slams me in the face when I least expect it—at a social gathering, in a meeting, out shopping with my mother, or going through airport security. I wonder if it will continue to escalate or culminate with some dramatic episode that lands me in the hospital emergency room or a psychiatric ward. No one ever talks about this part of the journey.

I have compiled a running list of symptoms. Memory loss, headaches, and hives. Blurred vision and numbness running through my limbs. Chest pains and palpitations. There is also bleeding and bruising. Out-of-body experiences. I am sitting above a scene of destruction watching the pieces of myself lying across the floor, like scattered parts of a jigsaw puzzle. I can't find my corners, can't figure out what part of me to pick up first, how to make the attempt at putting myself back together again. I feel dismembered, disoriented, unaware of my surroundings. I want to pick up the pieces, only my arms are missing and I can't reach over to grab anything.

My handwriting has changed. Before all this, I was a meticulous note taker. At meetings, conferences, seminars, lectures. Now I scribble like someone who might be suffering a muscular disorder or fine motor impairment. My scribbling runs along all sides and corners of the paper, words falling off the page, bleeding onto the desk or writing surface, leaving traces of me for others to find. I go back to read my sentences, and none of them makes sense. I cannot decipher my writing. Disfigured letters and phrases. Word salad.

I had a speaking engagement last night at the university. Petrified by the thought of having to make a self-introduction, I went through several sheets of paper trying to jot down pertinent facts about my past and present. Each a different rendition. I kept starting over, trying to rewrite the narrative. Who am I now, four years after losing Alex? Everything I said during my lecture sounded out of order and fragmented. The minute my presentation was finished, I walked straight to my car, wind and rain blowing through my hair, and imagined myself in the final scene of an old black-and-white movie with the credits running over my face.

Grief is conspicuous. I notice colleagues watching me from the corners of their eyes. Their stares make me wonder if I have overdone my makeup this morning, applied lipstick unevenly, smeared color erratically across my cheeks, turning myself into a comic book character. Maybe they're wondering, too. Who am I now and what is to become of me?

February 10, 2009

Armen,
I feel icy cold all the time. My hands, my face, my feet, my entire body. I want to scream. I want to run until I can no

*longer recognize my surroundings. Till I am in a real forest
and all I can hear is the wind, and all I can see are the tops
of the sequoias, old as the Bible, watching over me like quiet,
solid sentinels. I need a bodyguard; I want someone to keep
an eye on me, tell me that my limbs are intact. I want someone to pour me hot tea, tell me a good long story, give me a
happy ending.*

Nancy

PAPER OR PLASTIC?

February 17, 2009

Armen,

*The one thing I thought would remain constant was the
everyday activity of going to the grocery store. Something
so mundane and mindless was a way of resuming some
degree of normalcy. I had no idea what it would ignite . . .*

Nancy

I just needed cream for the coffee. I knew it wouldn't take long.
Although I didn't particularly feel like going out, I figured it
would be good for me. I'd been in the house for a week without leaving. It had been raining and overcast. So I got in the car
and drove about two blocks down the street to the grocery store.
I don't know what possessed me. I thought it was important to
venture out. I was going for one item. I'd be back in five minutes.

The doors swung open and I stepped into a place I didn't
recognize, though I'd been there a thousand times. Fluores-
cent lights glared, faint music played, people were placed like

actors, reaching for cans on shelves, dressed in uniforms, pushing carts, standing in lines, holding two things at once, seeming to be making some kind of comparison. I half expected that if I walked up and pushed on one of these people, he or she would fall right over, as though made of cardboard. Not real. But then, nothing in this place seemed real.

I walked down one aisle, thinking of all the aisles I'd walked down in my life: the hallway in the old house I grew up in as I dashed to my bedroom to hide, the wedding aisle as my stomach was twisting already with regret, the corridor leading from the labor room to the delivery room, walking up to accept a master's degree I never thought I'd get, strolling the cosmetic aisles of Sephora, giggling and comparing the twenty shades of brown shadow, holding each one up to Rachel's eyes and waiting patiently for her to decide. I wondered about my daughter's path on a gurney from the morgue to the autopsy room. I forgot to get a cart, or even a hand basket. I was taken in by all the colors, the lights, the packaging, the stimulation. I passed the baking items, sugar, flour, remembering that peach cobbler she loved so much. She had asked me to make it recently. Had I done that?

I turned down the produce aisle, started shaking, trembling uncontrollably, feeling exposed, naked, there amid the lettuce, the onions, the fruit. They were naked, too, sprayed with water. I saw myself lying among the fruit, splashed with icy water, startled, shocked with wetness, waiting for someone to come and put me in a basket, to take me home to some family, someplace where someone wasn't missing.

A stock boy passed me in the produce aisle, asking if I was finding everything all right. As he stood there looking at me, I had the sense that my face was not my own. As though I had been in some fire or accident, was disfigured, with people staring in horror. I can't remember if I responded. Of course I was not finding everything all right. Everything was not all right. My daughter was dead and I wanted her back and no, I was not finding everything all right.

Everywhere I looked there seemed to be order. The shelves were stocked with brightly colored cans or bottles or packages all arranged in some artificial uniformity, some organization that made sense to someone else. They were facing the aisle, arranged in perfect, neat rows. I was out of order, not knowing where I belonged. I had to get out of there, but I couldn't recall the way toward the exit. Then, of course, there was the cream. Had I gotten the cream?

I turned down another aisle and found myself amid jars and jars of baby food. My throat seemed to be closing shut and I was beginning to panic. I couldn't breathe. I looked to the right and saw strained peaches (had she started loving peaches as a baby?), diapers (she would tear them off and run naked through the house), small spoons (that she waved at me, flinging food across the table, giggling), pacifiers (she always had one in each fist).

I turned down the aisle that runs across the back end of the store, unfolding into a long counter of processed meats. Roasts, pork chops, chickens, salmon fillets, all packaged in shiny plastic, side by side, once running, swimming. The coroner was going to do an autopsy. What day was that going to happen? Or had it already happened? This day? Tomorrow? Next week? She would be cut apart, weighed, examined, notes would be taken, photos logged. Hard and cold on a steel table, bright lights hanging above her, she would be dissected. People who didn't know her, who had never known her, heard her laugh, felt her arms around their necks, would talk about her as they held their scalpels, just another junkie who screwed up. And here I was, looking at this never-ending line of meat, from one end to the other, quietly waiting. Their hearts had beaten at one time; blood had run in their veins. The counter seemed to be undulating, the packages slowly moving. Where the hell was the cream?

I stumbled down the aisle and grabbed the carton, now quickly heading for a checkout line. I found the cashier, who looked at me, stopped for a moment, and then asked if I was okay. I shook my head and handed him the cream. I looked up and saw a woman holding a baby in her arms. She was staring into my eyes. The next thing I heard was a voice asking, "Paper or plastic, ma'am?"

February 17, 2009

Nancy,
Without scaring the daylights out of you, I should probably give you a checklist of places that, for the time being, are off limits. Grocery stores are no place for the grief stricken, believe me. I'm sorry I didn't warn you. This otherwise friendly environment now feels like a haunted house. Stay

close to home for awhile, Nancy. Give the list to someone else.

Armen

CAR MELTDOWN

March 2, 2009

Nancy,
I left for work this morning feeling frazzled, disjointed. My car was my sanctuary for the good part of the day. How is it that even now, after four years, I vacillate from being a competent, coherent professional woman to someone who is feeling out of control and completely dysfunctional, back at square one? I'm not certain these episodes are prevent-able, and to be perfectly honest, mine have never asked for permission to intrude on my day. They arrive on their own terms whenever they wish. So I guess what I'm saying is, brace yourself . . .

Armen

I love my black gabardine suit. It fits like a glove, gives me an air of confidence, and acts as a second skin. I wore the suit delib-erately today, hoping it might harness my pain, keep emotions tucked in, and maybe even cushion me from this nagging sense of loss that is creeping up behind me like a giant tsunami. I have a full day ahead and can't afford to unravel. As the alarm clock sounds, I feel a tightening in my stomach. My jaw clenches.

As I drive to work, the early-morning clouds resemble gigan-tic pillows suspended in the sky. My thoughts drift to Alex. I fantasize about him outstretched, resting across one of them, as he often did on the sofa in our living room. Only now the gaunt look is gone, his brow appears relaxed, those tattooed frown lines erased once and for all. A silent voice quickly reminds me that Alex is dead. Reciting these words is never easy. Saying them this early in the morning is a sure sign that this day will become another journal entry.

By midmorning I am sitting at my desk with the feeling that my seams are showing. It's as if the hem of my pant leg has come undone, with threads and fabric now dragging along the floor, catching the heels of my designer shoes.

When I start to feel queasy, it's my signal to run for cover. I head straight for the women's restroom, hoping I can hide inside one of the stalls. I've come to prefer the one at the far end, marked HANDICAPPED. I enter, grabbing onto the walls, toes curling to grip the floor, and then lowering my head to get some blood flowing. I've mastered this ritual, but today I can see it isn't going to be enough. I will need to find refuge in my car.

The journey from the ladies' room, down two flights of stairs, and across the parking lot has reduced me to a state of muted hysteria. My gabardine suit suddenly feels like it is two sizes too small.

I bypass colleagues who look my way, as they often do, awaiting my cheerful greeting, the usual acknowledgment, but I look away. My legs travel in slow motion; my body refuses to cooperate, and the people around me appear to be carica-tures with bulging eyeballs and exaggerated features. I breathe rhythmically, inhaling through my nose, exhaling through my mouth. I need air. I can't seem to catch my breath.

A few more steps and I will be in the parking structure, fumbling for my keys, grabbing the car handle, opening the door, and collapsing into the driver's seat. There I will be surrounded by empty water bottles and unfinished sentences scribbled on scrap paper, remnant journal entries jotted during red lights. Also hiding beneath the floorboard are discarded tissues, crumbs from yesterday's lunch, and invisible memories piled under the litter of everyday life. I lock the doors as if that might shield me from further harm; I grab the steering wheel, press hard on the brakes, but it is too late now.

March 2, 2009

Armen,

I am comforted knowing it's not just me today. There is a feeling of being outside things, suspended somewhere from some distant vantage point, as though I'm watching all this happen to some other poor woman. I don't know if I can keep doing this for thirty more years. This is the closest I've come to asking to be taken to the hospital. Since you're in your car, maybe you can drive me?

Nancy

THE GRIEF HANGOVER

March 16, 2009

Armen,
Please rewind this night and give it back to me in a different
version. Hold me tight and tell me there is a light shining up
ahead. Everything I see is pitch dark down in this hole and I
am tired and scared. Promise me you won't let go and that
we can stay as long as we need to and not come out until
we're both good and ready . . .

Nancy

The barren night is a long shrill scream, stuck in my ears, a
siren that won't wind down. I know now how tired Rachel was;
I feel her exhaustion in every breath I am taking. She had told
me she didn't want to live anymore, that she was afraid to die.
But that last week in December depleted her more, and the
desire to be released from her mental cage was stronger than
the fear.

I lay here in the weight of the darkness, stuck in the guts
of the night, unable to focus on any one thing, hypnotized by
the ceiling fan rotating over my body for hours and hours. It's
a hurricane twirling above me, and I envision myself caught up
in the middle of it, spinning, not able to escape. I'm exhausted,
but I can't sleep. I'm starving but I can't eat. I'm insane, but I
can't give myself the permission to succumb.

I open my eyes to a morning worse than that four-day
binge of my youth, when I drank enough to kill a small pony
and had resorted to prayer, bargaining with the gods to let me

survive the hangover. Only I haven't had a drink in three days. I'm wobbly, head pounding, feeling tipsy, walking into doors.

Candles burn down, reminding me that the moment I'm in is only going to last so long and then there will be other moments, and more moments after that—all without her. I'd better find my balance quickly. I try to negotiate the rise from the bed to the bathroom, but can't visualize it. I could stay in bed all day and into the night, and the days and nights all start melding together in a blur, fragments of past experience, snapshots of memories circling my head. I am afraid of losing one of them, of forgetting. This is the grief hangover.

I close my eyes and see shadows of dark, light, half-light. I can't swallow. I know I have to get out of bed, but I can't feel my feet and I'm fighting the urge to throw up. And all at once I remember Rachel is dead. This is the new definition of motherhood. The dizziness, the disorientation, the sense of having lost something and needing to find it. This need is what forces you to sit up, when the nausea hits you and your mouth begins watering. You think you need to make it to the bathroom so you stand up, but then that feeling of having misplaced something returns and you forget the bathroom and start wandering and weaving around the house, looking for it. You can't remember what it was, but you are driven by a yearning, a longing stronger than anything you've ever known before. It's pushing down on you from all sides, like a vise. Like a labor pain you can't control, but can only brace yourself for. A pressure surrounding you, filling you up from the inside, forcing you out into your backyard, looking everywhere for this misplaced thing. What is it? You aren't sure because you are so exhausted you can barely keep a coherent thought in your head for one second.

If someone came to the door right now and saw me, they would think I had pulled an all-nighter, drinking myself into a stupor. They'd almost be right. But the stupor doesn't come from a bottle.

The thing I'm looking for all over the house, outside in the garden, in the garage, is not here. I remember now that the thing missing is not a thing, it's a who.

March 16, 2009

Nancy,

You are learning that this grief dance happens in cycles like a labor pain; it will crescendo and subside, ebb and flow, and the aftermath can be cruel, exhausting, and debilitating. You must become a skilled nurse at watching over yourself and knowing the signs, finding the right medication and treatments, or else the damage becomes irreversible. By the way, this thread that is unraveling you stretches over to me, too. You can call and in an instant I'll be by your side. Actually, I'm already there, next to you.

Armen

MONSTER IN THE MIRROR

March 29, 2009

Armen,

I woke up this morning, looked in the bathroom mirror, and didn't recognize myself. Like a scene out of Kafka's Metamorphosis, *I felt like I'd become some monster. I see my face in other people's eyes, in the way they respond to me. I had been sobbing late yesterday and remembered I had to pick up a prescription. I composed myself and drove over to get it. When I got home and finally looked in the mirror, I saw mascara running in streaks from my eyes down to my chin. Sometimes I don't know why someone hasn't called the police and reported a woman in despair at Walgreens . . .*

Nancy

As I moved through the hours and days following the news of Rachel's death, everything in the house changed, became bigger and more extreme. Something was happening to my senses. There was nothing protecting my internal organs, veins, muscles. My skin felt flayed, shredded. I resembled a reptile, always cold. I saw things that weren't there and didn't see things that were. My hearing was acute, like a wolf's. Everything seemed exceedingly loud—trains, cars, voices especially, the phone ringing. I wanted to use earplugs just to get the volume more normal.

I am a fragmented, Picasso-painting look-alike. A few of my friends have said, "I don't know anyone like you, Nancy." I ask what they mean, and they start describing some other woman they perceive as strong, inspirational, motivating, and I always have this surreal sense of myself in the past tense. I think, *Nancy used to be that way, but she's someone else now.* I've begun referring to myself in the third person.

It's late winter now; three months have passed. I find I can see through the middle of things, and through people. Perceptions are skewed. Colors are more vibrant. I am on heightened alert. My vision is microscopic, kaleidoscopic, telescopic, and has a zoom lens, too.

Everything in the world is suddenly on fire. I've been running a marathon, losing my breath, looking for a place to crumple, to rest. What is this incredible fatigue? Even if I do nothing but sit for hours, I feel as though I've been forced to march through hard terrain without food or water or sleep.

I walk into rooms and forget why I'm there. I begin a sentence or question and can't finish it. I look at someone and can't focus on what they're saying, or even who they are. I don't know how to plan the next five minutes of life.

I listen to the phone ring and can't answer it, or else I pick it up on the first ring, urgently needing to hear a human voice. I can't follow a recipe. I sit in the dark, unaware of the dark *as* the dark. There is so much internal darkness, I find it difficult to distinguish one from the other. I resort to going to bed at all hours of the day and night. I lie wide awake, afraid to close my eyes for fear of what I might see.

I am getting lines in my face from frowning so much. That furrow between the eyes, the lines around my mouth. They are etching my face with horror, disbelief, with sleeplessness, confusion. It's as though I'm watching myself change shape, from a human being to a series of reactions, emotional goo.

It's not just my face that has changed.

March 29, 2009

Nancy,

Don't fear the monster you see. Look her in the eye. Take her on. Don't let her deprive you of this once-in-a-lifetime journey, however fraught with terror. I'm sorry if she knocks you to the ground. She does me, too. In the end, her fury contains the power to transform us. Can't you see it starting to happen, already?

Armen

The Cemetery Club

COURAGE AND CLEAVAGE

April 6, 2009

Nancy,
Breasts. They are the epicenter of maternal love, of uncon-
ditional giving. As a baby, Alex loved to nurse. Was there
anything more satisfying than holding our children close,
providing them nourishment, and everything they needed
to stay alive?

Armen

To lose, to be lost, to be without or absent of something or some-one. Something that is missing. Like a mother or a breast or a son. I had faced losing one of my breasts in 1998. Today, April 6, 2009, I was back in the same waiting room, remembering . . .

It was a horrifying experience and I was obsessed with the possibility of being dismembered, deprived of something belonging to me. As I checked myself into the hospital, a nun in street clothes—face free of makeup, religious beads hanging from her neck—asked if I wanted her to pray with me. Had she noted the terror in my eyes? I extended my hand, as if I had already surrendered to a life sentence of radiation and chemo-therapy. We prayed. When they called my name, someone in green scrubs escorted me to the surgery suite for the biopsy. I pleaded with the surgeon not to put me under, insisting I had a high threshold for pain and only needed a local. I had to be in control.

My chest was burning like a raging wildfire headed straight for the part of the house containing one's most valued possessions. I braced myself for loss. They made the incision through the first layer of skin, and I could feel the blade digging deeper until it cut through the muscle so they could remove the pea-size lump. My heart pounded as if it were trying to leap through the opening. The room was quiet and freezing cold. I was trembling. In the next breath the surgeon's voice announced, rather matter-of-factly, that it appeared benign. She predicted I would be fine.

I had my annual mammogram this morning. It's been eleven years since the cancer scare and almost five years since Alex's death. That cold, chilled sensation returns. There is an odd silence and anxiety covering everyone's faces. The lady sitting across from me, maybe a few years older than me, revealed that this was her third follow-up visit for a suspicious gray shadow that keeps showing up on the X-ray.

"Not exactly the way my day was supposed to start," she moaned, trying to be cheerful and nonchalant, but I felt her dread as she flipped through the battered *Sunset* magazine that was lying across her lap. She was scared, as I had once been, both of us half naked, wearing those blue speckled gowns with mismatched string ties, much too short to ever form a bow. She kept talking so I nodded my head gently, almost as if I was rocking her in my arms. She then revealed she had recently lost her mother. Her sigh filled the entire room.

"I guess I shouldn't be so upset," she said. "At least I haven't lost a child. Can you imagine what it would be like to lose your child?"

"I've lost a child," I said. "His name was Alex." As his name emerged from my lips, another voice simultaneously called hers. She put down the magazine and stood up. Our eyes locked, neither of us knowing what to say, yet in this brief moment, we were so much greater than the sum of our parts: two women with four breasts.

There was one other woman in the waiting room, too, sitting just behind us. I was aware that she was listening carefully. As I was trying to catch my breath after the first woman left with the technician, this other woman leaned forward and whispered, "I've lost a child, too, a daughter."

April 6, 2009

Armen,

I haven't been able to stop thinking about these women you met this morning. It dawns on me suddenly that there are more of us in this grief club than I ever would have imagined. But even though there are so many, the journey remains lonely, solitary. This makes me wonder: Is there any way that we can reach out to them, Armen?

Nancy

LIFETIME MEMBERSHIP

April 12, 2009

Nancy,

A friend just sent me an article in a newsletter quoting a grieving father whose daughter died earlier this year. The note said, "I know you are not a grief collector, but I thought this might interest you."

One paragraph really spoke to me. It said, "To say that her mother and I were devastated doesn't begin to describe the helplessness, desolation, and utter darkness into which we were plunged by this event. Only a few people understand what we are going through: the deep depressions, the sense of being lost and purposeless, the aching wound that throbs at the slightest reminder of our daughter, and the daily exhaustion from wrung-out emotions. I view myself as a problem-solver, and another part of the helplessness I feel is the shocking realization that I can't do anything to make this better."

It's as though we are part of this exclusive club that no one ever wants to join—but once you're in, you're in for life . . .

Armen

Cynthia. Beth. Gail. Anne. Octavia. Terri. Liz. I'm sure I'm forgetting someone. The list keeps growing. These are women who are my friends. These women are also lifelines, safety nets, oxygen masks, each a quiet place where I go to unleash my pain and free the crazy voices that scream inside my head.

With them, I am able to rant and rave, vent and rage. And it is through our correspondence and conversations that each of us is learning how to breathe once again. Death has left us breathless. Empty.

I lost Alex and the floodgates seemed to burst wide open. Each loss has its own shape and form, its own story. Their children committed suicide, died of liver failure, perished in automobile accidents. A pair of them wilted and died of heatstroke; one died while living abroad. Two others died in airplane crashes, one died while playing the "choking" game, and the most recent member of the group, a young mother, lost her five-year-old son in the family swimming pool.

I began wondering if a halo of darkness was somehow permanently affixed above me, as if calling me to do something more. I felt besieged in the supporting role of grief counselor—attempting to play guide for a journey that had no particular road map or path, just unfathomable steps that I, myself, have barely been able to walk. But I was determined to remain vertical, petrified that if I avoided it in any way, down the road I would find myself locked away in some remote sanitarium. The choice to embrace my own pain and welcome the grief of others offered hope of survival and redemption.

I began corresponding with this group I now fondly refer to as the Cemetery Club, a stunning collection of women I met while attempting to navigate the muddy waters of my own personal grief journey. They, too, had buried children and loved ones. While we never held court at our children's grave sites, each of us felt close to the others' children—as if they were all part of the same graduating class or Scout troop. One woman named Susan sent me an e-mail a few weeks ago in response to a brief love note I had sent inquiring how she was doing. She wrote back, "None of us envisioned this much heartache."

During the past few years, I have watched too many deaths from orchestra seats. Casket after casket, one funeral after another, I felt like I was double-majoring in death. I helped write obituaries, organize tributes, and every single one of them forced me to relive my son's death until I wanted to vomit. My insides felt rotted. I had become an expert at planning funerals, memorials, tributes, and, as some would call them, celebrations of life.

These new sorority sisters keep dropping in front of my doorstep like casualties of war. Lying here, there, bleeding, crying, sighing, dropping in mid-step, unable to go one more inch. I look out my front door and see hundreds of them coming, walking slowly toward me. Eyes dark and hopeful, wanting anything at all, any elixir that can fend off the intensity.

April 12, 2009

Armen,

Could this elixir be found through community? I'm holding myself together solely because you've always shown up. I look at these sisters and wonder how in the world they are getting through each day. Who escorts their grief? We have to reach out, tell them we'll keep the porch light on all night, let them know they don't have to do this solo.

Nancy

The Mermaid Diaries

DORSAL FIN

April 22, 2009

Armen,

I was just in the kitchen and, for a split second, thought I saw the floor open up and this thing come shooting up at me, circling, moving higher, lower, but moving in circles around me. I looked up and it disappeared. How can everything seem so normal one moment, and in the next . . .

Nancy

In all the shark attacks I've ever read about, it seems the victims had no warning. They are described as experienced swimmers, and if they survived, they emphasized their sense of shock and surprise as something was clamping down on their leg or foot.

As much as Randy and I have always loved going to the beach and basking like seals on the sand, I've shied away from jumping in the water. I think it's been this fear of sharks, which represent something terrifying and mysterious lurking under the surface, and without warning or movement coming up from underneath and yanking me to the depths. I feel this same vulnerable fear now of being swallowed whole. Grading papers at my desk, it hovers next to my chair. If I'm with a friend at a cafe, sipping a latte or glass of Cabernet, it rises from a cement foundation, circles the table, eases back down for a while, only to erupt again if I shift in my seat.

At night it holds vigil near my side of the bed, and if I go for a walk in my neighborhood, I can turn the corner at any moment and there it is, appearing to slice through an innocent crack on the sidewalk, daring me to step over it. Sometimes it's only the very tip I see, almost a tease, letting me know it's near, and other times it rises up completely, showing me the top of its glistening body, gray and gigantic.

It reminds me of how slugs must feel when cruel little boys sprinkle salt on them, watching them melt away under the joke. Sometimes the attack is just as brutal.

April 22, 2009

Nancy,

I know it feels at times as if you're drowning, being devoured by sharks, but imagine that while you're swimming (and remember, I'm right there with you), we're being trans-formed, developing fins of our own, like mermaids—beauti-ful mermaids who can survive underwater, living among the fins. That's us—two mermaids learning to swim in the deep end of the ocean.

Armen

Breaking the Surface

May 2, 2009

Armen,

We are not women who are content to wallow in self-pity, darkness, bitterness, or fear all our lives. We are women whom others count on incessantly, who see ourselves on a continuum. The death of our children represents a defining moment. One moment on the continuum of our lives. There will be more. We are that Picasso, that fragmented, distorted painting, but we are driven to make meaning of our lives. We have fallen apart. But we are now in a unique process of putting these pieces back together again. They won't all fit neatly. The sizes have changed so they will fit differently. Some will hang over others, they won't all line up. This is not bad, though. We're changing shape, and this new shape may suit us. I'm cinching my life jacket tighter. I feel you with me. Thank you, thank you, thank you . . .

Nancy

When I was ten years old, I was swimming with a neighborhood chum. He was a few years younger than me, and our mothers were friends. We were splashing in the deep end of our pool and he suddenly slipped below the surface of the water and disappeared. Everything in the next sixty seconds happened as if in slow motion. I saw his mother rise from her chair, her hands waving; she was screaming. My mother started screaming, "Nancy, Nancy," but neither of them jumped in. I instinctively dove, vertically, through the water.

I imagined my feet as fins. I could see him on the bottom. I grabbed his trunks, pulled hard. He was heavy, and I was a skinny kind of kid. Heaving with every ounce of strength in my arms and body, pulling him toward me, I looked up through the wavy liquid and could see the sun's rays filtering through. I was getting closer.

Then he jerked, pulling me down. He was panicking, trying to stand on top of me. I could feel us both going down again. My breath was running out. It seemed like hours, but somehow I grabbed him around his chest and pulled him right up next to me, reaching for the top of the water, finally breaking the surface. I got him to the step where he started throwing up water. Our mothers ran to him, pulled him out of the pool.

Then his mother, after calming down a bit, walked over to me, lifted me out of the water, buried her head against my cheek, and sobbed, as she felt me shaking and gasping. She didn't let me go for about five minutes. All she could say was, "Thank you, thank you, thank you." I knew then there was something in me that was a survivor. I was strong.

We who have lost children are part of a strange elite. Like pushing through the back of the closet in *The Chronicles of Narnia*, we've fallen through to the medieval forest beyond, uncharted and frightening terrain. But the children were obsessed with returning to that closet world. They felt pulled in its direction because they knew the lessons to be learned there were somehow also connected to the sacred, and to the forbidden.

I have been trying to visualize surviving the loss of my daughter ever since it happened, and what that survival will look like. Surviving is not a place you eventually arrive at, but a path you walk. It is hallowed ground. There seem to be two paths: One is the path of surviving, where staying open is crucial. I visualize myself a wet noodle, bending with the emotional current, letting myself conform to the shape of my feelings. The other is to give in to total collapse, to despair, that Miss Havisham syndrome where one gets stuck and can't move forward.

Everyone has advice for the grieving. Assumptions they make about time, memory, healing. We are steeped in clichés: *The first year is the hardest. It gets easier with time. You're going to be okay. You need to have closure. You need to get back in the saddle.* You need, you should, you ought. Many of us find it gets much harder with time, not easier. There is no such thing as closure. We are so uncomfortable with things we can't fix, with people we can't rescue.

Just like breaking the surface of the water, we have to find a way to emerge from this, take in the air again. It's as though we've been falling through time, through space, through memory, childhood, dreams, to the deep end. And if we don't locate that ray of light soon, the danger is that we'll stay down there.

May 2, 2009

Nancy,
You are being pulled into the undertow. I wish I could assure you that life will be better tomorrow or the next day, because it may. But this phase may also linger, like the stench of

death, like the bills that come after the funeral, like the notes you have to write for all the flowers, like the memories of Rachel that appear randomly and take your breath away. If you need me to meet you someplace, run away with you, hide in a closet with you, or just e-mail you constantly, I will do that. Let me be your life jacket. Hold on to me.

Armen

Till Death Do Us Part

For Better or Worse

May 14, 2009

Nancy,

I know we haven't delved much into the impact this nightmare has on marriage—but all of a sudden I am remembering how horrible it was during that first year, to feel like I could not touch the person I loved the most. Dan was suddenly so far away—we were traveling the same journey but miles apart. I remember sensing he was trying to reach for my hand while I seemed to be pulling it away; maybe it was so numb I didn't even know it was there. I felt tired, depleted, so much so that even if I could have felt him reaching out, I would have been too exhausted to respond or reciprocate. Being alone seemed like a better solution. I had nothing to give back. No one really ever understands that. You feel dead—just like your child.

Grief is the ultimate test for a marriage—you and Randy may need knee pads to crawl through it for a while, find a way to simply exist together. It can get pretty messy . . .

Armen

During the first months after Alex died, my husband and I tacitly pointed fingers at each other—never deliberately or with the intention to hurt, but in the course of our conversations words would emerge, leaking anger and resentment—words like *controlling, narcissistic, enabling*. We blamed ourselves, we blamed each other, we blamed the schools, society, friends, the times. Maybe life had been too easy. But now it was anything but. We had fallen into the snake pit of grief, and it was hard to claw our way out.

I wondered if our marriage would survive. I remembered our vows: in sickness and in health, for better or worse, till death do us part. I wondered if that included the death of our child.

As I look back on all the tripping we did—the blame game, the silence, the profound sadness that filled our household, and the divergent ways each of us coped with Alex's death—I understand how the death of a child can obliterate marriages, even strong ones like ours. Dan retreated into a private world of silence, burying himself in work, building a wine cellar, and drinking himself into a stupor. I wasn't far behind. Alcohol was a quick fix, layering a blanket of fog over the pain, anesthetizing our grief, allowing us to at least exist.

I wanted to talk, write, understand. His grief was more private, internalized. Our timing was off. We lived in separate universes for a couple of years. I had a therapist. I prayed he didn't take a lover. Both of us knew that the marriage was fragile and that we were walking a tightrope that could easily drop either one or both of us to the ground. The normal instinct to help your mate was gone. Just as I had felt worlds apart from Alex, I began feeling separate and apart from my husband. This realization frightened me. I couldn't go down that road again. Thankfully, neither could he.

And so we tried to dance together all over again. With or without music, we moved differently, at our own paces, with tolerance and compassion. Inevitably, we stepped on each other's feet, stumbling, offending, smashing, and hurting. It was exhausting, and we took turns sitting the dance out. While one partner was on the dance floor, the other was leaning against a wall, watching.

Most of the time we felt as if we were back in junior high at those awkward gymnasium sock hops when you're waiting to be tapped on the shoulder. But mostly, we wished we were invisible, back at home, away from the crowds of spectators and freed from the sick feeling that no one would ever want to dance with us again.

That's what the grief dance feels like, only a thousand times worse. But we got through it. Or should I say, we're getting through it. We know we're committed and trying but realize the dance lasts forever. There's no simple choreography.

It's taken us a great deal of time and patience, but we have begun listening to music again, swaying our bodies to its rhythm, accepting each other's arms around shoulders, waists. Even when we are not exactly in sync, we know we're dancing again.

As each note plays, and with every step, I sense the eyes of the world watching to see if Alex's death will make or break us. It has done both. There have been long, lingering periods of estrangement—from loved ones, from our selves. When the teetering shakes us off our feet and takes us to the ground, the fall delivers some sacred message to those standing by us, especially our daughter, Danielle. The journey of life is steep and plagued with twists and turns. I see her eyes watching with intensity to see how this chapter ends. Or begins all over again. We are frail, but more human now. Grief cracks the heart wide open.

May 15, 2009

Armen,

My cousin last week asked me how it could be that any two people could make love again after losing a child. She said, "I mean, it's the way you created that child, so each sexual encounter is just a cruel reminder of that moment when she was conceived. How do you do it?" I'm being reminded in this moment how sex is so symbolic of life, of regeneration, of intimacy, of love, of letting go, of being able to receive, to give, to be a partner. The more I hear you speak of Dan, the more I realize Alex's death resulted in strengthening your marriage. Having to pass through the fire either melts you, or illuminates you.

Nancy

IN SICKNESS AND IN HEALTH

June 8, 2009

Armen,

I just picked up the manuscript and threw it across the room, thinking that it was all a bunch of crap. Who am I fooling? There is no meaning in this. I forgot my lines,

Armen. The prompter went home. I'm out on stage, stark naked, without a line in my head, staring at an empty theater. The show is over. I can't see my way out today. She is gone, she is never coming back. I can't see value in anything. Not my marriage, my husband, my other two children, my house, my life. Everywhere I look today I see a white erase board. Fade to black . . .

Nancy

My husband, Randy, has worked as an emergency room nurse in a small rural hospital for over a decade and tells about how many of his tribe have PTSD. That's why, when the director of emergency services, his boss and best friend, hung himself in his garage six months after Rachel died, he wasn't entirely surprised. When you work in an emergency room, nothing surprises you. You are trained for the unexpected. And then Randy had already been dealing with a wife who was only sleeping at best one night a week, eating every other day, and then only a cup of cottage cheese. It was hard for me to get even that down.

My doctor had given me sleeping medication but I wasn't taking it regularly, and I was drinking myself into a coma nearly every night. My memory was shot. I had no interest in sex or anything that reminded me of life. I felt dead, and worse yet, I didn't care.

One night a young girl arrived at the emergency room, strung out. She later died of the overdose. Randy came home that night, more exhausted than I'd ever seen him. He was leaving one ER to come home to another. I didn't have dinner ready and hadn't even given it a thought. The house was dark. He found me sitting on the floor in a corner, staring out a window. What he did in the next moment is emblazoned in my mind. He put down his keys, kicked off his shoes, and sat down on the floor next to me.

Then he lowered his head in the same way people do when they are praying. He didn't say one word, but his presence communicated that I was not alone—and that he was honoring the grief, honoring where I was in it.

In the months following Rachel's death, everything seemed to be put on hold. The usual rhythm of life ceased, and normal rituals like eating, sleeping, talking, making love, going out, became impossible. I would think I could get through something as familiar as going out to dinner with friends, but the first night we tried it—with friends who in fact had lost their son only one month before Rachel—I had to excuse myself and ended up fleeing the restaurant, running all the way home on my own. Randy got home shortly afterward, horrified and worried about my safety.

Rather than rebuke me, he wrapped his arms around me and let me be where I was. He's never left, although God knows I expected it. So many nights he says nothing at all, understanding my need for silence. He is quiet and sits next to me, but not too close. He doesn't ask me questions. He doesn't tell me what I should do or be or feel. It's as though he has taken grief on as a new partner in our marriage.

For six months now, he has cultivated and nurtured a colorful garden in back of our home, planting forget-me-nots, tulips and other bulbs, plants, flowering shrubs, placing wind chimes that sing in the breeze and fountains that ping with watery sounds. He is creating a peace garden, somewhere I can go to regroup, pick myself up off the floor.

I don't know if our marriage will be one of the strong ones, or whether we will survive this, but I know we're taking this on, one moment at a time. As he said yesterday, "A promise is a promise."

June 8, 2009

Nancy,

Take your time. I'm here, too. Sometimes reality slaps you in the face and it stings like hell. Another layer of numbness is peeled away. There are so many layers, Nancy. Before it's over, you will be standing naked looking in a mirror, not sure if you recognize the person who is looking back at you. I love you no matter where this thing takes us. Even if this becomes the last entry, the last page of the book, and it gets buried in some trunk off in the closet for a few years, nothing would have been wasted. I am fuller, richer, better for having traveled to Griefland with you for five unimaginable months.

Armen

The Dragon Stitch

June 18, 2009

Armen,

This absence stretching out in front of me forever is starting to seep in. Each day, each hour, presents a new opportunity for accepting life, without Rachel. This is another one of those honest moments. Perhaps that's all death really is. Brutal honesty. When death happened, I was first sucker-punched by it, though it seems to me now like this strange welcoming committee—eager to usher me in, standing still, silent and waiting patiently for me to acknowledge it . . .

Nancy

The more than two years Rachel spent in Utah at a private high school designed to help drug-addicted teenagers was an exercise for me in surrendering control. I was separated from her for seven months before I was allowed to see her for the first time after she was admitted. According to the rules set up by the school, she had to earn the privilege of having contact with me. The months were torture, but at the time there seemed to be no choice but to place her there and leave the rest to the professionals.

Then, one Thursday, her therapist called. Rachel had earned her first visit; I could come that weekend. Without much planning time, I drove the long road to the school, through California, Nevada, Arizona, and finally Utah, and the tiny town with the population of forty-seven where the facility was located. We had one day together.

When I picked her up, she was ecstatic. She raced toward me from across the long yard where her name had been called. She hadn't known I was coming. Her eyes danced, she wore her famous huge grin, she jumped on me, wrapping her legs around my back, nearly knocking me down. We collapsed in each other's arms. She was crying with joy.

She told me she had learned to crochet. Since there wasn't much to do in this little town, and we had to stay close by the school, we went to a craft store where I bought her skeins of chenille yarn in burgundy and gold because she wanted to make an afghan for our living room.

A couple of years later, when she came home from the school, she proudly presented her gift. It was gorgeous. It was gigantic. The chenille gave it a plump appearance, with each stitch looking like it had been infused with air. It was so stunning that I draped it across one of my living room couches.

Her sister, Jessica, who also crochets, noticed the unusual crochet stitch. Rachel said it was called the Dragon Stitch, and she'd learned it from the other girls in the school. But nobody we knew seemed to know how to do it. We couldn't find it online anywhere, and Rachel couldn't explain it; she had to show us. I couldn't follow it, but Jessica finally got it down by observing and practicing. Rachel liked the Dragon Stitch because she said it gave the optical illusion of having two sides when there was actually just one.

Since her death, I've left the afghan draped across the couch, right where it's been every day since she gave it to me. Yesterday I stopped and stroked it. It seemed to beckon. I put it up close to my face and looked deep inside it, into the intricacy of the stitches themselves. I could see the complexity, the beauty, the uniqueness of each stitch, the intensity of the colors, burgundy and gold. Those were the colors in her hair. I could see her, feel her fingers pulling the yarn taut, weaving it out and around the needle, connecting the threads, each one perfect. She had touched every single stitch with her fingers. I could see her stroking the finished product, holding it in her hands. As though it emerged straight from her palms. I imagined all the conversations she had with her roommates while she was working on it. The interruptions, the hours passing. The unraveling stitches here and there when they got messed up. She would have redone every stitch till it was just right.

On an early summer morning, six months after her death, I stood in front of the bathroom mirror, felt something looking at me. I turned my face to the open window. On the screen perched a gigantic dragonfly. Its wingspan must have measured five inches across, the colors iridescent burgundy and gold. Although I didn't feel compelled to disturb or touch it, I watched it throughout the morning; it didn't move for hours. Both of us, it seemed, were hypnotized. Transfixed. Somehow together.

Nancy,

We are living in the land of lost and found. We lose them for a few minutes, hours, or days, and then we find them—in the sky, in a Mother's Day card, in an afghan, in a photo album, or in a sentence or paragraph of an unfinished letter. Suddenly they are with us again. But not for long. I see Alex and Rachel as I type these words. I visualize their faces as screensaver images staring right back at me. I know we are trying so hard to hear their voices, interpret their words, understand their reasons for running away from life. Wrap yourself and this day in the afghan, Nancy. Find enchantment in the wings and stitches that whisper her name.

Armen

Confessions of a Gypsy

June 24, 2009

Nancy,

I'm not sure if I've ever mentioned this before, but right before Alex died, I started questioning everything about myself. I entered this period of feeling like a complete impostor. A fake. By day, I masterminded a six-figure job and had total control of my environment. By nightfall I would return to utter chaos, never certain if the house would be standing. The only thread holding me together during the ordeal was the vision of a gypsy, twirling in the sunlight, layered in bright colors, jewel-toned hues of passion and laughter. Recently, I have sensed her withering away, dangerously close to death. Help me revive her, Nancy . . .

Armen

One day, about three years ago, while driving home from work, the radio played something by Carlos Santana. I can't remember the title, but the ethnic rhythm and smooth, sensuous tempo caused my body to gyrate, my arms fluttering wildly as if readying themselves to take flight. My fingers curled up like a belly dancer, and even my hips lifted off the seat cushions of the car. This went on for the entire song, culminating with a riff that brought a downpour of perspiration emerging from even the most private crevices of my body. I noticed myself in the mirror and barely recognized the Armen staring back at me. This Armen had fire in her eyes.

That night, while Dan made love to me, something strange happened. I could not shake a morbid image that haunted my thoughts. He was making love to a corpse. The corpse belonged to me. Dead and lifeless, my airbrushed smile was attached to a hardened, ceramic body—a mannequin. Artificial and empty, scared to death, a faint shadow emerged, ghost-like, running from the scene. Fleeing, she left everything behind, discarding a life, a marriage, a former self she no longer wished to associate with. I realized this shadow was me, needing to be someone else now. Someone new. Someone less dead.

Engulfed in an awkward, inconvenient moment of passion, I traveled back to another place in time when this same sensation had first taken hold of me. I was a college student, in my early twenties, trapped between midterms and dead-end relationships. I retreated to the stacks that day, a place reserved for hard-core studying in the darkest corners of the university library—a perfect spot for last-minute cramming and hiding from worldly creatures. I loved it there—I could bury myself in the musty pages of old books, stare endlessly at neurotically outlined notes, and create one fantasy after another of a life I had yet to discover.

As I made the ascent to my favorite hiding place, something caught my eye, strategically hung at eye level, on the second-floor landing. The poster carried an enticing invitation to study abroad. Never having stepped foot outside California, I was surprised by what happened next. Goose bumps erupting, I grabbed an application, stormed down the stairs, sat under a shade tree, and began filling out paperwork.

Four months later, carrying the red Samsonite my parents had given me for graduation, I climbed three flights of stairs leading to some primitive dorm located in the south of France. For the first time ever, I met the gypsy—a blanket permission slip to push my own limits. We became friends somewhere between Marseilles and Milan. At first I found her to be a bit nerve-racking. I skipped classes, packed overnight bags, boarded night trains to remote cities, and gave her free rein to be my tour guide. I discovered a whole new world with her. Most of all, I discovered myself, falling in love with this new version of me.

Now, thirty-five years later, I wonder what ever happened to the gypsy. Something must have caused me to place her in protective custody, guard her with my life, stow her away until it might be safe for her to emerge once again.

Back in the confines of our bedroom and in a moment of sheer panic, I began fidgeting to find a pulse at the base of my neck. There was a sense of urgency to know that I was still breathing, still there. Someone had ripped off the oxygen mask, the life support that had barely been keeping me alive. I was crossing over some mystical precipice, wanting to hand myself over to her.

Dan was still touching me and I felt nothing. Only cold. The same way I felt when I rested my hand on Alex's hardened chest before they closed the lid of his coffin. They didn't like that I was touching him, pressing down on his heart, as if it might resuscitate him and the nightmare would end and we could all just go home and resume life. Maybe if there had been just a few more minutes, a little more time. But they were anxious to whisk us off in the limousine.

I wasn't ready to go, but no one would listen. Tonight, in a moment of exhaustion, I was still prying his coffin open for one last look.

I'm tired of faking it. So tonight there is a different kind of climax. I lay still, staring up at the ceiling. The ceiling is dropping, falling so close to my face that it becomes the roof of my son's coffin. This time, I'm inside, too. Death has taken its toll. The metamorphosis begins. I am shedding my skin, breaking free from the pain. A gypsy emerges.

June 25, 2009

Armen,

Late-morning madness . . . bear with me here. Remember Viktor Frankl's Man's Search for Meaning? *I opened it this morning to a page talking about a person's worthiness to suffer, which led me to my own fantasy about our worthiness to suffer these losses. I saw two celestial beings up in the heavens talking about sending souls back to suffer.*

"We've got to send someone down to deal with the death of her son. Whose turn is it? Who's the worthiest?"

"Well, we've got a gypsy from the medieval period who has been signaling she's ready to live again. We could send her down. Let's call her Armen in this new lifetime, what do you say?"

"Yes, but is she worthy?"

"Yeah, I think so. She was a writer in the last lifetime, cerebral, a great dancer, singer. I don't think she'll waste the experience."

"We'll have to pair her up with someone else. Who else do we have?"

"Okay, here's a witch that was burned at the stake in 1625. She didn't have a chance to finish suffering in the last lifetime, and she's a great candidate."

"Why do you say that?"

"Chick's always looking for meaning. She wouldn't shut up the last lifetime, which is why they burned her. And she was always avoiding standing still, so the two of them would be a perfect pair."

"Got it. You think these two will make it happen?"

"They're the best we've got."

And so began our magical, marvelous, obsessive, artistic alliance.

Nancy

Passport to Griefland

July 4, 2009

Nancy,

When we first disembarked here in Griefland, we were stunned and in shock. We arrived without reservations, accommodations, our luggage had been lost. We had no grasp of the language, people, or customs. To make matters even worse, we had no map, because no one had ever developed one for Griefland. So here we find ourselves, lost in a land of strangers and strangeness, with no itinerary and no Sherpa. But we are thick-skinned Amazons and we have each other through this rugged, unforgiving terrain . . .

Armen

Griefland will never make it to the front pages of *Travel + Leisure*. Unlike other destinations, there are no how-to-navigate manuals, no five-star hotels, no Michelin guided tours for those destined to explore it. The landscape is treacherous and steep. But neither one of us by now was a stranger to the mountain ranges of unthinkable altitudes, rock formations sharp and slick, forged from nightmares and forbidden scenarios. Cliff hanging and daring adventures had become commonplace.

We arrived at Griefland's borders at different times, almost five years apart. The dates on our passports are stamped with distinction: July 17, 2004, for Armen and December 25, 2008, for Nancy. We felt an inexplicable bond, nevertheless, as if we might have met at the same departure gate or while boarding the plane headed for this new and never-before-seen destination. Although I had technically arrived before Nancy, it was as though I was seeing this place for the very first time.

As our friendship evolved, we found ourselves alluding to this new place where we now resided. We decided on the name *Griefland*, as if to be modern-day explorers stumbling upon an undiscovered frontier. It became the sole place that felt natural, almost primordial, a safe haven for our sadness, rage, and jet lag.

"We're somewhere we've never been before."

"Hold my hand."

From that moment on, we were traveling partners. There was no turning back. Griefland became the region where we had permission to grieve out loud. Surrounded by inhabitants who, like us, knew the face of death and had also endured profound loss, we noted the country was plagued with silence. No one was proficient in the language. We seemed to be the only two making discourse.

People were flocking to Griefland. One by one, we discovered the faces of others who had crossed the borders, many wearing veils, making it difficult for us to see their eyes. We felt lonely and secluded and decided perhaps it was up to us to create a language for this country. It was time to lift the veil of darkness. Unlike many of the others who grieved quietly and stood still and immobilized, we chose to venture out.

Griefland became a powerful metaphor to describe the landscape. We found caves that allowed us to hide, avoid people, reflect in privacy, make noise, or sit vacantly in an effort to heal our deepest wounds. We located dark tunnels that twisted and turned, that threatened to take us down to sewers and underground passages.

There were monsters that inhabited these places, and we learned to be on our guard. Even when they took us down, we figured out how to get back up while bleeding and broken. We climbed razor-backed mountains and walked through valleys, got lost in tangly forests, on wide beaches, and on open seas, stared into deadly tornadoes and exploding volcanoes, and barely escaped dangerous quicksand marshes.

There were strange weather patterns here, too. Rain, blinding sunlight, clouds, windstorms. Through it all, we stuck together and explored each avenue and detour. We knew if we didn't, this country would have eaten us alive. But at the same time, as challenging as the terrain was, it somehow offered great comfort. Beauty in vibrantly colored meadows, cathedrals of waterfalls, and glittering dragonflies. The moon became a welcoming escort, oftentimes accompanying us and offering light and promise when our eyes were weary and bloodshot.

As we continue to push ourselves through the environment, realizing that we will carry Griefland with us for the rest of our days, we discover surprising sights; Griefland is also breathtaking and majestic. Most visitors will never tell you this. Perhaps our experience is different because we are traveling this journey as a pair and are able to experience these hidden treasures with less fear and more wonder.

Together we stumbled upon the Griefland Cafe, a fantasy inspired by van Gogh's *Cafe Terrace at Night,* a favorite print we both have hanging in our homes. It became and still remains a place of refuge, always open—twenty-four hours a day, seven days a week, especially on holidays. We meet there often. A benevolent waiter in a finely pressed tuxedo, always nurturing, has a candle burning, red wine poured in sparkling colored glasses, and warm bread in a napkin-lined basket. Like a good mother, he eagerly cares for us when our feet ache, when we can't walk another step, when we are melting down, beyond exhaustion. He keeps our table open with a RESERVED sign on it, and his eyes are always watching for us. This image of the Griefland Cafe will forever be our touchstone, something to focus on when we are in the darkest of caves. Good thing we discovered it early.

While the Griefland Cafe is only a metaphor, its imagery remains powerful. The cafe lifts us up when we are on the ground, and provides a mental and emotional emergency room to recover. It represents unconditional love, the bonds of friendship, nurturing, deliverance. Whether we navigate the rocky environs, endure the brutal weather patterns, or find peace beside the quiet pools of water, we keep returning to the cafe, knowing it offers the strength to get us through another day.

Sometimes we feel like natives, more comfortable in Griefland than in this other world where we are often forced to wear masks. This place reeks of honesty and has become a bizarre kind of sanctuary, a strange combination of Oz and purgatory, safer than our "real" world. We created a language, a collection of words and descriptions, some spoken, others transmitted via eye contact or hand gestures, and eventually became fluent.

We recognize there is no getting out of Griefland. Meltdowns are a common everyday occurrence. It's normal in Griefland to see people sobbing, breaking down in restaurants, collapsing on their front lawns. If you are a native of Griefland, you accept these scenes as commonplace, offering a simple flower or touch. Rather than ignore the grieving, we know here in Griefland that the appropriate response is to wrap our arms around the bereaved, hold them close to us, let them know they are not alone. We're all here, like a family, bringing food, nurturing the wounds, easing the person back into the present tense. Nothing they could do or show or say could make us feel any different about them. The ultimate prerequisite to going to the next plateau is shaking hands with grief, taking it on, looking into its face. Calling it by name.

July 4, 2009

Armen,

I've been thinking that at some point in this journey, it may be possible to cross over into another realm, another part of Griefland—the interiors, like the darkest parts of Africa. We venture deeper as we gain more knowledge, as we put more words to this place. We are making our way toward the capital, which may be hard to reach, but once we make it I hope we will find that we can live with this huge crack running down the center of us.

Nancy

The Language of Silence

July 5, 2009

Armen,

Randy and I will be leaving for Monterey in an hour. While I'm on the beach, or at night, when we leave the bedroom door open and I can hear the waves crashing against the shore, or in the morning, when we go on our long walk down the path that runs next to the sea, you and I will still be connected in time and space. It seems to me, Armen, that from now till one of us dies first we will always be there, hanging in the silence, in that space between words, waiting for each other . . .

Nancy

When Rachel died, the greatest silence of all, the silence of death, engulfed me. I lay down in it like a field of poppies and let it envelop me for a solid week. I didn't listen to music, not to voices, television, the radio; I didn't talk on phones; I didn't talk much at all. If someone came to visit, it was fine as long as she didn't say anything or expect me to speak. Noise was a knife slicing through the silence I needed to help me accept this presence of the absence of my child. It's as though I needed every ounce of quiet.

Today it is early July and I am watching dry leaves hanging from trees outside my dining room window. There is a hot breeze flowing through the branches. The leaves are swaying, bumping against one another. The sun is relentless, burning a scar in the sky. I am shrouded in silence. The house is quiet, and I am alone. Only the occasional humming of the refrigerator is audible. I have come to know that silence is one of the major dialects in this new landing place.

A simple phone ringing now will undo me. I take it off the hook. For today, this unworldly hush is all I can listen to. It is the sound of reflection, of memory, of photographs, of loneliness, of redemption, of reinvention. It is the sound my daughter now makes for me. Words no longer have use. They are only inadequate reminders of what can never be expressed. What can never be completely shared.

My eyes drift across the table to a frame that holds an image of her. She is grinning from ear to ear, embracing her brother, who is looking down at her. This image seems to have arrived from some other universe, beyond life and death, their faces looking out at me from the boundaries of another time. Another photo shows all three of them, seated in a row, a professional picture that her sister orchestrated, a holiday gift for me that year. What year was that?

Outside a black-and-white cat slinks across the street, stalking something. Or looking for something. It seems we're all looking for something. I'm in suspended animation, at the bottom of a pool, frozen and staring through the water toward a full moon that is shining through wavy patterns of liquid. I feel heavy, my limbs weighted down with memories and regret. I could stay down here forever, I think. The weight of the silence surrounds me, fills my ears. I am consumed by this white space, this gap between the words.

I can't locate my voice; my tongue catches, wilts in my mouth. I try to make a sound and there is a chokehold on my throat. I search for some word that can capture this rawness, this feeling of being diffused into space, splattered into a million pieces against eternity. I yearn to put words to this sensation. But I know nothing I say will change anything, nothing I say will describe her as she was in life, nothing I say will depict the way my stomach is rocking like a ship cast about in a stormy sea.

And in the calm I am able to hear the smallest of sounds—the purr of the cat curled around my foot, the ticking of the hall clock, the faint harmony of the wind chimes echoing from the garden. What I really need is for everyone and everything to stop. I have to pay attention to the internal sounds, the new rhythm of my heart. The inner voice that quivers and tells me I am surviving, whispers to me when it's time to get in the car and leave, to catch my breath, envision an entire day of life moving forward without her. It's only in the silence that I can hear this voice. The stillness is the only thing that mirrors my internal state, where everything has gone dark, becoming more familiar now than the world of sound had ever been.

July 6, 2009

Nancy,

I wonder what would happen if we could be still long enough to hear silence. It has a voice all its own. A voice that few are accustomed to listening for. It might feel awkward at first, even empty, like a blank page. Imagine the lack of distractions and intrusions, and a new ability to listen for sounds that rise up from the soul. A symphony of silence.

Armen

Alex, Is That You?

July 17, 2009

Nancy,

As time pushes forward, Rachel will undoubtedly greet you in many unique ways just as Alex has done with me. As a seasoned traveler, I have been on the road for more than five years now, so this kind of outreach has become familiar and commonplace. I'm confident Rachel will be finding you soon. After all, she was creative, mischievous, and playful, much like Alex. It's quite possible they'll go to the ends of the Earth to make us smile again. We never give up on them, do we? Not even now . . .

Armen

Not that any of this death dance makes sense. You suddenly arrive in Griefland, certain that you have crossed into another dimension, and the results are both frightening and comforting. As your body finds its way into its new altered state—where side effects, out-of-body experiences, aches, and pains seem to deluge you all at once—the outer world also seems to toy with you. In my case, five very specific things began happening with frequency—so much so, that they were hard to deny or attribute to chance or happenstance.

Alex had a passion for lizards. He had a menagerie of them as a young boy, and when he grew older they made regular appearances in all his drawings. Maybe he liked the way they could lose and grow body parts, reinvent themselves. Perhaps it was their sleek movement and ability to slither, or their chameleon quality, or their ability to wiggle out of a tight spot that made him love them. He never outgrew his attraction to reptiles.

The morning after he died, the strangest thing occurred. As I walked from my bedroom to get some coffee, a lizard appeared on my kitchen floor, staring straight at me. The lizard and I both froze, and I knew I needed to do something to prove to myself this was not a dream or delusion. I walked quietly to the cupboard below my sink, grabbed an empty pickle jar that was leaning against the box of dishwashing detergent, and unscrewed the lid while lowering it to the floor, all the while gently whispering to the lizard to crawl inside.

If this was Alex, it was the first time he was not openly defiant, because the lizard required little coaxing to crawl right in and make himself at home as I screwed the cap firmly into place. *Now what?* I wondered. I decided to show Dan, which I did, even though he was partially comatose from the Ambien-induced sleep state prescribed by his physician. A few moments after showing him my catch, I felt guilty, as if I might be trapping my son (who was now mysteriously transformed into a lizard) somewhere between home and the afterworld. I walked slowly outside the back door, lowered the jar to the ground, and set him free. This gesture somehow gave me comfort, as if Alex had returned to say good-bye one last time.

Lizards continue to make their appearance on billboards, television ads, in the yards of friends and relatives—just about everywhere I go. I have learned to smile and say hello. Last week I went to visit a friend in Woodland Hills, and as I was leaving her house to drive home, there, perched on her front door, was a lizard. The lizard followed me down the sidewalk until I got into my car, and then went on his way, disappearing into the flower bed. He had made his presence known. No need to belabor the issue.

There are also power outages. They started a day or two after Alex died. First it was the garage door opener. Then the lights in our bedroom went out. The battery in my new car died. Twice. The mechanic said it was highly unusual and impossible to explain. That's the same thing my jeweler said when my (new) watch battery died. We sent it off to the manufacturer; they replaced the battery and serviced it and three weeks later it happened all over again. I haven't done any research on this sort of phenomenon because truthfully, I'm not so sure I am a believer in this paranormal stuff. But all I can say is that it happens regularly, consistently, and often enough for me to scratch my head, thinking, "Well, maybe."

I see his letters—A's and X's—in the sky. This skywriting, as I fondly call it, emerges from cloud formations. Well, that's the logical explanation. Remember the scene in *Wizard of Oz* when the Wicked Witch writes the words SURRENDER DOROTHY in the sky with her broom? It's like that—only the sight of these letters fills me with hope rather than fear. Alex was a writer; I have convinced myself that if there's a way he can send me a note saying he's close by or hanging out in the heavens, this would be his way. I know it sounds crazy; it does even to me.

Almost as crazy as the 17s that are everywhere. Alex died on 7/17. I am not much of a fan of numerology and have a hard enough time remembering my own Social Security number, telephone number, and my husband's and children's birthdays. But everywhere I go, there are 17s. They show up as flight numbers when I book plane reservations. When I go for fast food, my order number is almost always 17. The server hands me one of those plastic numbers to place on my table so they can bring me my food and there it is, a "17" to place on the tabletop. The 17th is also the date my new granddaughter was born. The list of 17s is long and endless—but more than anything else, it allows me to feel his presence. The more 17s I see, the more I feel Alex.

And finally, there are the Kohl's newspaper ads. Shortly after Alex died, Kohl's Department Stores arrived in town. In perusing the weekly pullout advertisement, I noticed a young man who might have been Alex's twin brother. This handsome kid had Alex's exact physique, the same muscular arms, the high forehead and semi-shaven head, the dreamy eyes, and has become a weekly visitor as I sip my coffee and read the morning newspaper. Some days he appears in casual attire; other days he is all suited up as if he might be going to a business meeting or social event. Some days his pose is so Alex-like that it takes my breath away. My friends and relatives have started noticing the ads. I clip them faithfully now, as if they might someday be pasted into a scrapbook to chronicle Alex's life had things worked out differently. Some days he is a student going to college; other days he resembles a Wall Street stockbroker or attorney. However this has come about, it gives me a glimpse of Alex in living color, exactly how I had dreamed he might look as a healthy, happy, and thriving young adult.

July 17, 2009

Armen,

I ran into a young woman at the pharmacy today. As she shifted from one foot to the other, her arms folded in front of her, I recalled how much Rachel hated her body, and this girl seemed just as vulnerable. She was standing directly in front of me and turned around. I smiled. She said, "Your eyes are so beautiful . . ." I thanked her and told her she was beautiful, too. She lowered her eyes, locking them on a spot on the floor. They were huge, almond-shaped, and brown (like Rachel's). She didn't say anything, but I called her attention to how much radiant energy she exuded, and then her name was called. As she walked away, she grasped my arm, and said, "Thank you." I watched her walk away. As I stepped up to the window, I was glowing inside, feeling peculiarly as though I had just had a conversation with my daughter.

Nancy

Leap of Faith

August 4, 2009

Armen,

Something happened to me this morning.

I was alone in the bathroom, putting on makeup, the light on. It suddenly grew dim, this light right above my head. No other lights did this; the whole breaker didn't shut down, it was just the bathroom light where I was standing, and it went out . . . in slow motion. I closed my eyes. When I opened them, my left eye was filled with blood, as though I had broken a blood vessel. Then when Randy got home, he told me that last night about 2:00 a.m. he woke up suddenly and felt a presence by the side of the bed. He turned his head and Rachel's face was right next to his. He insisted she was right there. I don't know if this is real—or the product of acute hysteria . . .

Nancy

I've never had faith in anything or anyone. Maybe it's the by-product of the tragic relationship I had with my mother, maybe it's just my own neurosis, but I have never believed in God, in a life after death, or even in most people I know. So when Rachel died, I never went looking for her. I didn't feel singled out for persecution. Even in the first moment after I received the news,

I didn't slip into denial or look around for someone to pin the blame on. I knew exactly what had happened and why, and I knew no one person nor any one thing could have prevented it—except for Rachel herself to have made a different choice. But I also knew she couldn't do that and had tortured herself for years trying. Nothing would change the outcome.

This sunlit morning as I sat at my computer writing, Rachel's name appeared in the instant messaging box as being available for a chat with me, so I figured someone must have hacked into her account. Although startled, I didn't believe it could really be her. There was a logical explanation somewhere. Watching the cursor pulse a heartthrob in front of me, I typed into the box, "I'm here." No response. I tried again, still no response. For a fleeting second, I thought if she were trying to contact me, she knew exactly where to find me. We were always e-mailing each other.

But it was the act of typing into the box that struck me. Why did I do it? This nonbeliever, this heathen who has never believed in the divine, never believed in an afterlife, never believed in any grand design to the universe, was typing out a message to someone dead, adrenaline pumping through me like lightning, desperate to believe it could be possible. And I tried twice. I repeated myself. I didn't get an answer, but I did gain something else, something entirely unexpected.

August 4, 2009

Nancy,

This journey causes us to teeter, cliff-hang, nose-dive. In the darkest hours, we hold on by our fingernails. But there are other moments, too, filled with marvel and magic, giving us reason to believe in something bigger than ourselves. Whatever "it" is helps us navigate the pitfalls, the blind corners, the jagged edges of our grief. Imagine for a moment that Rachel is by your side. Let her in, Nancy. Talk quietly, feel her touch, don't be afraid. This leap of faith may in turn bring an unexpected wave of calm that allows you to breathe again.

Armen

I Wonder if the Palm Trees
Are Dancing

Logan Dominick was born on May 28, 2003. Weighing in at seven pounds, ten ounces, he was healthy and beautiful, an exact replica of his father, Alex. It was hard not to fall instantly in love with him. He personified the purity and goodness that was once my son. How can I do justice to describing the mixed emotions that were going through my mind as I entered the hospital's maternity wing? On one hand, I was reliving my own labor and delivery, remembering the joys of motherhood, the thrill of holding new life in my arms and never wanting that feeling of bliss and happiness to subside. But here I was now, feeling out of place, making my entree into the world of grandparenthood, the timing awkward, strained, and inconvenient. All I could think about was my own son, the one who at twenty-one years of age was emotionally broken and fragile, in a state of perpetual infancy and regressing with the passage of each new day. Wanting to protect him, I imagined marching into the maternity ward for the sole purpose of having him surgically returned to my womb. That's where he belonged now. It was the only place I knew he could be safe.

But instead I tiptoed into the nursery to meet my new grandson. Although I was crazy about him from the instant our eyes locked, I felt split in two. Alex was dying a slow, visible death, withering away right before my eyes. The stronger Logan grew, the weaker Alex became. Sadly, the transition was seamless.

By the time Logan took his first steps and could mouth the word *dada,* his father had grown unrecognizably thin, catatonic, speechless. He was also forbidden to have contact with his son. This broke his heart, but not enough to stop the substance abuse. I kept waiting, hoping he might rise to the occasion, but instead his own despair seemed to offer more license for self-destruction. Looking back on it all now, our lives were wildly out of control on all levels but one. There was this child.

And each time I held him, I knew he was carrying both the burden and the legacy of his father's life, one filled with seeds of greatness, potential, and hope.

We buried Alex the following July, leaving Logan to the loving watch of his mother, grandparents, aunts, and uncles. Together we would nurture his spirit, give him room to grow, and find ways to keep Alex's memory alive. Much like his father, Logan would see the world through his own unique set of eyes, taking notice of things most of the rest of us never see.

A grandmother has the privilege of cultivating rituals no one else is privy to. Together, that's exactly what Logan and I did. I don't mind admitting here that I felt a special connection to him, like the bond I had once shared with my son. We could travel to uncharted territory that was beyond what most people talk about. Logan is a conversationalist, a deep thinker, very pensive. Much of our time together is spent drifting off and away, as far as our imaginations can stretch.

"I wonder if the palm trees are dancing," he said one afternoon as we were driving to my house for a few hours of play. Our house overlooks a lake and is surrounded by palm trees. Most children are drawn to ground-level things: insects, rocks, dirt, things they can touch with their hands. Here was this tiny person, barely two years of age, face turned toward the sky, asking thought-provoking questions, and pondering the universe. On more than one occasion, he would ask me one of these questions, and at about the same time I would feel a slight breeze sweeping behind my neck, right beneath my hairline, as if someone was whispering secret words behind me. Logan would seem wildly attentive in these moments, as if he could see things happening outside the margins of normal vision. It's made me wonder if he can maybe see his dad. He sits for hours and watches the trees swaying in the wind.

Together we have created an array of outdoor rituals using water as a reflection pond, the patio as a place for contemplation or quiet conversation. There is another spot, the bottom step nearest the dock, where we make our wishes known to the fish, ducks, water creatures, and anyone who might be boating in the vicinity. Whether one of us yearns for the sight of a rainbow, the downpour of summer rain, a full moon (his "Bella Luna"), or something outlandish and outrageous—say, a bevy of butterflies or dragonflies putting on a ballet in the sunlight—we discover this magic together. We also collect rocks that Logan has convinced me possess special powers and are made expressly for us. To this day, we throw them into the lake, sending endless wishes up to the heavens. During all of these moments, I feel Alex's presence.

I had imagined having more time to grieve Alex's death. But life tugged at me, repeatedly. First Logan was born, and then my daughter's two little girls, Arden and Ani, made their entrance into the world. The trio of them forced me to move on, move forward, and keep moving ahead. Maybe that's the answer. Death makes you want to be still. Alone. It seduces you into thinking you want to stand still until your legs give out and you fall to the ground, sinking into the earth to be with your buried child. But you don't. Because like the palm trees blowing in the wind, you are destined to dance again.

August 22, 2009

Armen,

You are coming back, aren't you? You are earthbound, claiming life on new terms. Negotiating the journey. Do you have any idea what you have given me just now? A way of seeing how life can keep going on despite this loss. You have shown me that I need to keep my focus skyward.

Nancy

Where Is She Now?

September 14, 2009

Armen,

I must have hit every stop sign on the way back from the university. It made me think of all the stops I've made in my life. I stopped my marriage when I'd had enough of the misery. I stopped my job with the newspaper when I knew it was time to move on. I stopped enabling Rachel when I recognized I was contributing to her self-destruction. And then that ultimate stop. That stopping of the heart. I imagine what her last heartbeat sounded like, felt like. Did she know it was her last? Did her heart gradually slow down, or just come to a crash landing? I wonder whether she knew she had crossed over the line and screwed up, or whether she didn't have the strength to scream for an ambulance. Or whether she thought to herself, Thank God, it's finally over. And just closed her eyes forever. Do you think she knew how much she mattered to me, Armen?

Nancy

It's mid-September, 3:00 a.m., and I'm outside staring at the stars, the blue-black night drop, and the breeze is kicking up. I'm in the back garden. Nothing looks familiar here, though this is a spot where I sit frequently. Rachel sat here, too. We would often talk together in this place. Where is she? Where has she gone?

We were the closest when I was carrying her. She'd literally taken up residence in my body, and she didn't want to be born. She was nearly two weeks late and I had to be induced. Rachel seemed to want to bask in that warm security forever. She seemed to be fighting with each contraction, fighting for her right to stay put, to stay in the dark, warm spot that meant comfort and home.

Rachel once gave me a card that said: *A little girl, asked where her home was, replied, "Where Mother is."* She often repeated this line to me as the years passed. And even in her last year, when she lived with a woman who agreed to look after her while she was completing her rehab, she quoted it frequently.

We talked several times a week, and she would say how close she felt in that connection. She would call me on the full moon, ask me to step outside and look at it, in exactly that same moment. She would ask if I saw a certain line in it, a shadow. When I said yes, she would giggle, saying she saw the same shadow. She told me if we were both looking at the moon in the same instant, that meant she was home. But where is she now?

In the blackness of night, often outside, I sit and talk with her again. I tell her I am surviving, as I promised her I would if this ever happened. I ask her to give me a sign that she is okay, that she has everything she needs. In those late-night moments, when I'm alone and the sky spreads out in a dark blanket all around me, her presence is almost tangible. I think I see something out of the corner of my eye, passing across the garden. Maybe she's closer than I can imagine. Yes, she's come full circle. She's right inside me again. I ask her questions. I ask her why it was her and not me—why she could not have been stronger and believed in herself; I tell her that she was lovable, worthy. I ask her what would have had to change to prevent this outcome. The answers, they say, come through other mouths.

September 15, 2009

Nancy,

Why was it Rachel and not you? Because you are the stronger one of the two. I remember when you wrote this to me at a time when I was crumbling in despair. You boldly wrote me that we had been chosen to carry the load. They did not have the stamina, Nancy. Alex and Rachel had short, intense fuses. They could set the world on fire but their private flames were predestined to be short-lived. They perhaps somehow knew that. We will never know for sure. But what I do know is we must do the heavy lifting for all of us.

Armen

Chipped Nail Polish

October 13, 2009

Armen,

As I was getting dressed for work this morning, I looked down and noticed chipped nail polish on two fingers of my left hand, mirroring my internal state, another part of me peeling away. For most women, this would be no big deal. They'd finish getting ready for work. For me, it was a full-blown emergency. I cannot bear losing one more piece of myself. I cannot stomach seeing one more thing chipping, falling, or peeling off me . . .

Nancy

I am getting ready for classes in front of my vanity mirror, the same one Rachel used to primp in front of several years ago. It is ten months after her death. She saw her reflection in this glass just as I am doing now, assessing her image, putting on rings and bracelets, never feeling beautiful. My jewelry box is open and arrays of bracelets, necklaces, and rings are spread out in a fan in front of me. The daily ritual feels different this morning. I start by putting on my wedding ring, and that's when I notice that even jewelry presses heavy on my fingers, wrists, neck. I try on a bracelet and it feels like handcuffs. I'm claustrophobic now. The necklace feels like a noose.

Ten months ago life was another color. I was teaching literature, planting bulbs, petting a Siamese cat, barbecuing steaks on Sundays, calling my three grown kids every week, having Chardonnay with friends, taking walks, running sprinklers. In an instant, I felt cast as a character in a film being shown in slow motion, rewinding, fast-forwarding, stopping in the middle of a scene, leaving me on cliffs.

Twenty years from now, as I look back on this hour, I imagine it will seem as though time is still distorted. It has stopped somehow, and I seem to be viewing life as through a portal or alternative dimension. In this new place, the clouds have changed shape; they look sinister. I find myself standing before a classroom full of students, and although we've been meeting three times a week for nine weeks now, they look like strangers. Every single person, thing, sensation—even an evening breeze— is an ordeal.

Then, once again, I'm shaken back to the present, staring at my chipped polish.

October 14, 2009

Nancy,

As I write this, I am noticing my nails are unpolished. This is so out of character for me that it makes me wonder if it is intended to be part of some transformation. Must we be stripped down to nothing, no polish whatsoever, before we can accept this new color of life?

Armen

Time of Death—Forever

November 4, 2009

Armen,

A new month begins without her. There is a continuing sense of absurdity surrounding all this. I can't get my head around the permanence, the finality. I remember when she was born; I couldn't envision my child dying. I feared it (maybe all new mothers do?), but I couldn't visualize how people survive it. And it amazes me that I haven't just burst into flames. Some days it feels like I will, and then it almost comes as a surprise that I'm still standing at the end of the day. But there is a strength that comes in that moment, too, when I'm still standing. Something is turning over in me . . .

Nancy

How can it already be early November? It sometimes feels as though I'm inhabiting a place or time before any of this happened. Some mornings I wake up surprised to find myself in this particular house. For one fantastic instant, I fancy I'm back in the house where Rachel was born, in the country, the Sierras rising in front of me against a golden backdrop. It's always fall there, in my mind, and reddish brown leaves are swept across the expansive front garden.

People have told me that time heals all wounds. What I'm learning is that time is passing, but healing is not some magical process that occurs simultaneously. And actually, I'm not entirely sure what "healing" means. Does it mean you won't think constantly about the person you still love who has died? Does it mean you will stop feeling dead yourself? Does it mean resuming routine activities and not feeling nauseated all the time? Does it mean being able to hide better?

I'm beginning to realize the similarity to being given a diagnosis of diabetes, or AIDS. There is no cure, no healing to speak of in the truest sense. Once diagnosed, you are afflicted all your life. You live with the disease and experience the process every day until the day you die. The best you can hope for is to be so self-aware that you become an expert in caring for your condition, giving yourself the right dosages of insulin or meds every day. It's not so much about healing as about management.

Since first reading the certificate and noting the time of Rachel's death, 10:00 p.m., I have been struck by how clocks and watches continue ticking. I notice beginnings and endings now. The beginning of an hour, a minute, a season. It's November 4, and fall has arrived. I'm noticing that at birth, a life begins, and at the moment of death, it ends, and only then, in its ending, can we see the whole thing complete, and clear. The entire sphere of existence that was Rachel's life, from watching her hug her first friend, to singing her first song, to having our final conversation, eyes locked on each other across a table—it's all there.

It's 9:00 a.m. At the end of this last hour, I look behind me to see what happened. That was an hour I felt the surging of my heart in my chest, as though it would leap right through my rib cage and make its mad bid for freedom. I looked out a window and saw life—two cars drove past, a dove landed on the lawn and cocked its head to one side, a cat pounced on a pile of leaves, the sun's rays glistened on the desk in front of me. It was silent in the house. The phone did not ring; no one came to the door. The quiet filled me like water pouring into a glass.

It's true she died in one discrete documented moment, which is gone forever and irretrievable. It exists on an autopsy report, on a death certificate. And yet she seems to be dying over and over again in each moment that passes. As though I am just receiving the news in each new hour, like a rerun of a tired film, the scene revolves repeatedly through my mind. How the phone burned my hand, how my body froze before the words were even uttered. It was in that moment when I began to see other vestiges of myself falling away, like leaves in autumn.

Eleven months ago, I saw my daughter for the last time. Since her life ended, I have been seeing her differently, as a child, running across a green blanket of turf. Jumping on a trampoline. I hear her laughter. I feel her arms around my waist, her fingers pressing against my back, just between the shoulder blades. I feel her body against my chest, breast to breast, with no air in between. So tight, like a gift-wrapped present. I can feel her breathing, exhaling and inhaling as we stand in the embrace. I see all these things lucidly, as though they are happening again in real time. I want to turn off my mind, but seeing that can't be done—and seeing there are probably many years ahead for me, which will pass sometimes quickly, other times slowly, or will stop dead in front of me—I meet each hour with a flimsy promise that I won't hide out from death, that I'll breathe it, taste it, shake its hand, invite it in.

And when it crosses my threshold, I also realize I missed my daughter before she died more than I miss her now. Because now, it seems, she is closer than she was in life. She was running so hard, as if in a marathon, so fast that I couldn't catch her except in rare moments. It was often in the quiet, when she wasn't talking, but just sitting next to me, that I sensed her own grief. I've asked myself if I will ever be able to forgive her for choosing death over life. And it's in this moment, when I feel her so near, that I can whisper an unequivocal yes.

November 4, 2009

Nancy,
There is a point when you do start breathing again. It may be fleeting, but it gives you hope. And one day you laugh again. You desire your husband again. You can grocery-shop and maybe even walk down a baby aisle without losing it. These will be defining moments when oxygen fills your lungs, the sky appears blue again, and you can see Rachel's smile without having a meltdown. It's a slow and subtle transformation.

Armen

Still Life

December 2, 2009

Armen,

I went to buy a friend's daughter a baby gift. Her pregnancy is a reminder that life continues even after death. I roamed up and down the aisles of newborn clothing in a familiar stupor that occurs when my emotions collide. I stopped at the sight of funky newborn jammies, the kind with feet in them, and covered with peace signs, well suited to Alex and Rachel's personalities. I visualized us chasing them through the house in younger versions of ourselves, delighting in their fearless and independent spirits. And then I walked out to my car, exited the parking lot, took two wrong turns, got lost and disoriented, and eventually found home. Do you realize the holidays are almost here and I have no idea how to meet them this year. If I don't surface again today, I know you'll understand . . .

Nancy

It's early December 2009, the one-year anniversary of Rachel's death, and my neighbor is teetering on a ladder as he stretches the lights across the front of his house. When he finishes this activity, he'll put out that plastic candle that lights up from within and greets visitors at the front door.

This year Christmas will feel different. It was on that day she made her departure from this world, so instead of visualizing her old fairy stocking she loved to investigate on Christmas morning, or instead of decorating as I usually do, this month feels as hushed as a morning fog, quiet, as though someone hit a mute key on the computer of life.

This is the month I've been wondering about for nearly a year. That marker that reminds me I'm still alive, but frozen—a still life—that I've survived the step out of time into the realm of no-time. Where the frost that sweeps the lawns with glistening white has infiltrated my body and soul like a virus, moving through each vein and artery, to the ends of my toes. I am frozen from the inside out.

I have endured the seasons of this year, and they are shifting once again, piles of crimson and yellow leaves scattered across the lawns down the street, swishing around my ankles when I shuffle through them. This must mean fall is in the past. I feel death in the seasons, even as I feel it under my skin. It's becoming more and more familiar. I know I am still Nancy and still breathing because Armen keeps writing to me and I know Armen must be writing to someone. If she believes I'm here reading her letters, then I must exist. But then why do I feel so absent?

In the middle of the night, I awake to a body that is trembling, quaking, as though it's imploding, a psychic earthquake with my heart wedged in the middle. I hear trains in the distance outside my bedroom window, and the faint glow of my neighbor's lights seeps through a crack between the window and the blinds, casting a vague silhouette against the far wall. I try to grab hold of the light source but it changes shape and fades as the hours pass. Sometimes it looks like a flower; other times it resembles a vase, moving from a living thing to something now that is still, hard, inanimate. The dark used to be just an absence of light, or a kind of shadowy space, but not now. Now the shadows tremble in front of me like flames flickering.

I remember Christmases past. Images of trees, ribbons, laughing, wrapping paper torn and scattered across the living room floor, cookies, hot chocolate, kisses, hugs, games. I see Rachel's corkscrew curls in all these images, as though they are trying to make their way back into a barren landscape.

It is not Christmastime in this hour. The fog thickens like a good soup, and hugs me in anonymity, in blissful quiet, trying to lure me into a season whose arrival I fear. I don't know how I will get through the rest of December, but there is one certainty—Decembers will have to be lived differently now, just as life will be different. I will navigate those waters, those holidays, those seasons, each in their own time. I have to. Because Rachel is out there somewhere, waiting for me. So is Armen.

Nancy,

You have every right to be falling into the cracks of the earth. This is her month. Go ahead and fall to pieces, crumble and dissolve, cry and scream, sob and mourn. Reality is not going anywhere, and even if you let it out of your reach, it will return. Let yourself melt into this first winter, Nancy. Let yourself go dormant like the seedlings that are waiting to break through the earth. They can't push through the soil without making it through the first frost, can they?

Armen

Silent Night

December 25, 2009, 12:14 a.m.

Nancy,

I can feel you both so strongly tonight. I see her corkscrew curls. I feel your love for her. Thank you for the honor of getting to know and love Rachel through you this year. It has been my year of magical healing, too, Nancy. Whatever thoughts are playing in your mind throughout today—whether it is an instant replay of Rachel in real life as a toddler, child, teenager, or troubled young woman—I know the dominant feeling will be of missing her, wishing you could hold her one more time, shield her from harm, and guard her for eternity. You have reminded me time and again this year of your incredible love for your daughter. On this first anniversary of her death, may you be mindful of the life and energy she has given you every single day of 2009 to chronicle this love story.

I know—how can it be one entire year since the phone rang?

Armen

December 25, 2009, 7:17 a.m.

Armen,

It's as though a gray fuzz has fallen in front of my eyes, changing all my senses. A part of me feels numb, but also tingly, as though I'm inhabiting some place outside the ordinary realm of existence. I'm sure you'll hear more from me as the day unfolds . . .

Nancy

The moment I opened my eyes, I could feel the strangeness. It was like a new lens coming down in front of me. I pulled on some faded jeans and a sweatshirt, kissed Randy, and told him I needed to go out for a drive. I said I would be home soon. It was 8:00 a.m.

There are some moments where we feel ourselves surrendering, clicking onto autopilot, where the repetition of a simple facial movement like a smile becomes tedious, banal. Where we perform the motion merely to respond, to feel more normal. Grasping the steering wheel, I pushed my foot down on the gas pedal and drove. East.

Old routes don't die in our memories easily. I have forgotten many details of past relationships, heartbreaks, misunderstandings, but the route I took to get to my summer home in Shaver Lake, the route I took to pick up my kids from Fairmont Elementary, the route I took to walk from junior high school to my parents' house when I was a teenager—these roads are inscribed in my soul. Every path, every mailbox, every canal is a vein in my body, a road leading to some vital part of myself. The turnoff was right here.

My car knows where to stop. It stops on Brehler Street, the lawns dusted in frosty white, trains of smoke curling from the tops of chimneys. People were home, kids were tearing open boxes, ribbons and bows strewn across floors, warmth emanating from kitchens.

I roamed the perimeter of the property, praying no one would emerge with a shotgun and keep me at bay while the police were being called. There it was. The outside gate that would lead to the playroom, the trampoline, the area of the garden in which we would set up the Slip 'N Slide every summer for the end-of-school swimming barbecues, where all children, parents, and teachers were invited. I see Rachel running at full speed and jumping off the diving board into the pool in some former version of this place. It was such a wonderland.

I look absentmindedly at the clock, which is striking 11:00 a.m., and realize I've lost all track of time, just like a dead person, living outside the boundaries of humanity. I drive the long road home, past what is called the Blossom Trail around here, the skeletal almond and peach trees standing in barren rows. In the spring, though, they will sprout pink and white flowers, their perfume permeating the landscape for miles.

Randy is stirring something in a skillet when I step through the back door into the kitchen. He looks up and in that deep, strong voice tells me he's making something fun for dinner. I move toward him; our eyes lock. He knows, and I clutch him next to me, feel his heart beating wildly against mine. Only one thing matters now. As searing as this yearning for my beautiful daughter is, in this one solitary moment I am grateful for so many things—for Armen, for our magical alliance, for this man with the velvet voice who is a human pillow, taking the brunt of the fall, making sure I am safe wherever I land. Most of all, I see that life and death are intertwined—with all the horrors, miracles, magic, wonders—together they strengthen the human heart.

December 25, 2009, 9:06 p.m.

Nancy,

All I could do today was visualize you, me, Rachel, and Alex frolicking in some high-definition overgrown forest with a make-believe castle or chateau, a huge tree fort or place they could hang out in while we sat in the bejeweled writing room with that long table, bottles of wine, crystal goblets, a worry-free, timeless environment where we would write till forever with no interruptions. At some point the waiter would arrive, summon the kids inside, and we would sit together and eat, catching up, word for word, on the journeys that have taken place during the past year. My heart aches with you tonight, missing what once was, but appreciating what is now, and what most certainly will be in the days and weeks to come, because one thing is for sure— we're still standing, fingers and hearts intertwined, moving forward. Before I turn in for the night, let me once again embrace our friendship, this alliance, a friendship that only Rachel and Alex could have initiated. They were the catalyst of what we have penned as perhaps our greatest lifework. At the stroke of midnight you will have crossed over to Year 2 of Nancy's Healing Journey. And I'll be here in the morning, to make sure you are okay.

Armen

Duet

December 28, 2009

Nancy,

Sit down, darling. I have amazing news to share. My daugh-
ter, Danielle, is pregnant. What is even more magical is that
there are two babies. Just as you and I were laboring over
the completion of this first draft, her babies were being con-
ceived. Would we call this life imitating art or simply a mira-
cle? And get this—she is having a boy and a girl . . .

Armen

My mother recounts a lovely tale about the falling star she saw on the night she went into labor with me and my sister. She had no idea whatsoever that there were two of us growing inside her. But she desperately wanted a baby and, as they wheeled her into the maternity wing of Saint Agnes Hospital, the sight of this bright light suspended from the heavens prompted her to wish for twins. A few hours later, we were born. Although she has shared this story hundreds of times, each time I hear her words, I am reminded that anything is possible.

I loved every moment of my own pregnancies, and although I wasn't blessed with twins, Danielle and Alex were only twenty months apart and very close as siblings. When Alex was born, Danielle couldn't take her hands off him. Her brother's arrival sparked the foundation for her nurturing instincts. I would lay him in his crib to nap and walk to the other side of the house to cook, clean, or work on a project. She would immediately go missing in action. Invariably, I would find her hoisted over the crib and snuggled up against her baby brother, arms tightly wrapped around him.

She acted as his guardian and mentor, and was the consummate big sister—protective of his every move, taking him by the hand, teaching him her favorite nursery rhymes, and consoling him when he was sad or scared. He adored her and never resisted her bodyguard tendencies. Besides, he was usually clever and convincing enough to steer her into his world of creatures, cartoons, kittens, and crayons.

As they grew older, I delighted during those times when they would wander into each other's worlds, sometimes to help with homework, other times to analyze the drama of boyfriend–girlfriend relationships, or simply to talk after lights went out as best friends often do. They were different as night and day, and yet there was closeness, a connection, an inexplicable bond between them as if each had a front-row seat into the mind and heart of the other. Almost thirty years later here she is, the sole survivor, with two daughters of her own and on the verge of giving birth to twins.

As an identical twin, my sister and I also shared this closeness. We possess the exact DNA. This past year the medical school at Danielle's alma mater, USC, invited us to be part of a twin research study. One morning, we spent hours spitting saliva into a sterile beaker, all for the sake of science. The lab technician, a husky woman in her early thirties, proctored the test. She reminded me that twins hold many answers to the mysteries of life. After she left, I gulped down a gallon of water and then sat in awe of the bond I share with my sister. We are mirror images, two halves of a whole, and there is this mystical layer of intimacy that must have jelled when we were tightly embraced in utero. Besides Nancy, she is the only person who knows me inside out, can finish my sentences, and catch me when I fall. I have witnessed her powers throughout this grief journey. When I weep, she aches. If she rejoices, an unexpected grin appears on my face. There is a thread that runs through the middle of us that joins us at the hip, heart, and on a much deeper level—at the core of our souls.

During many of our late-night e-mail conversations, Nancy and I have imagined that Alex and Rachel might have been the best of friends, almost twin-like had their paths crossed in this world. As we have exchanged stories and memories about their lives, we have come to believe they were, indeed, kindred spirits. Perhaps in another time or place, they would have moved mountains together, even taking on some of the highest plains in Griefland to spare us the climb.

Throughout this unanticipated grief journey, we have often commented how reliving these experiences and committing them to paper has resembled labor and childbirth. We have endured aches and pains, utter exhaustion, and moments of exhilaration. Together we have conceived and delivered a new life-form through the collection of essays we have penned. We note at this final juncture that we are now in a state of perpetual transition—at last crossing the borders of Griefland, knowing there is no turning back—weary-eyed but filled with hope as we breathe deeply, inhaling and exhaling, cheering each other on with the same encouragement and support one witnesses in a delivery room.

A dear friend of mine asked me recently if I am afraid for the soon-to-be-born twins, worried that something may happen to them someday and bring my daughter heartache. After all, it's a perilous world and a challenging time to bring children into it. My answer was an unequivocal no, because hasn't it always been? I refuse to live in fear. The joyous and even harrowing moments of parenthood give our lives contrast and texture. At the end of the day, I would travel these steps all over again.

Shortly after Alex died, one of my dearest friends wrote to me that all babies enter the world perfect. As parents, we love them unconditionally, we protect them with all our might, and we give them wings so they may fly to the destinations of their dreams. And we pray for their safe arrival. Tonight this is my wish for Danielle and her babies.

December 29, 2009

Armen,

I want to tell you about the beautiful dream I had last night. I saw two small beings, clasping hands. They were in a tight, enclosed area and their eyes were closed. I must have been seeing into the future, Armen. Although these babies won't be our children, they'll be near us, and I predict they will grow up looking after each other, supporting each other's dreams. In hearing your news, I think it's fair to say we've come full circle.
Nancy

Round-Trip

December 31, 2009

Nancy,

I have more thrilling news. I've been invited to do a series of motivational lectures for educators at an international conference next year. Italy is calling me. Today I received two invitations from the head of schools inviting my husband and me to multiple-coursed dinners while we're in Florence. I RSVP'd favorably to both of them and I'm already salivating for pasta and gelato, and wine, of course. I even came home and took out my leopard suitcase. My inner gypsy is alive and well, here with me now. She's feeling naughty and irreverent. My presentation notes are all in my head and I know where I'm going for a change. I am dedicating this trip to Armen and Nancy, to show the world that indeed there is life after death, joy after despair, and destinations beyond Griefland. I love you, Nancy, and tonight, I am sitting on top of the world . . .

Armen

It is the start of a fresh year, and I am being called upon to do speaking engagements and other presentations to motivate, inspire, and engage others in our lofty mission to help children reach their potential. Whenever I am asked to do these kinds of talks, I instantly return to memories of Alex in elementary school, brimming with curiosity, the first child to raise his hand, volunteer to help the teacher or a classmate. He was a passionate learner. One of those kids whose hands are always bouncing in the air, eager to share an idea or perspective. Remember the movie *The World According to Garp*? Alex, too, had his own distinctive view on the world—he had opinions and ideas about everything. It was *The World According to Alex*. The thought of it all is making me smile this morning. No one can take away those precious days from my memory bank. Nobody.

This morning I spoke to an audience of nearly a hundred and for the first time in five years, I had full command of my senses. While there was a bit of a formal introduction, I had other things I wanted the audience to know about me, a context, enough background for them to know of my passion and respect for good teaching, the value of lifelong learning, and what constitutes compassionate leadership. More than anything, I wanted to model the message I was trying to impart, determined to make eye contact throughout my speech, something I have been unable to do for quite some time now. I'm so tired of looking down at the floor or over the tops of heads as I speak. This morning was different. The room was small and well lit. Sets of eyes were only inches away from the podium and my soul. My senses were wide awake. My hair was on fire. I was alive again. The adrenaline was pumping, but not from fear. It was a moment of self-return.

"Good morning. My name is Armen. For the next hour I want you to look at me. There will be no note taking. No cell phones. No distractions. Just us. A hundred of us, each with the power to nurture, cultivate, and maybe even save the life of a child." By the end of my first sentence, there was a pulsing energy that everyone could feel. I even noticed someone who had been leaning against the door, ready to make a quick exit, stand up rather attentively.

Then I did something daring. I turned over my notes and stepped away from the podium, a prop I have used for the past five years as a hiding place for my squirming hands, the knots in my stomach, the tremors in my legs, as I have awaited the ground to break open, sucking me in, making a complete scene while my audience watches me disappear into the bowels of the Earth. Grief stripped me of confidence. But I was different today. I knew it the moment I entered the room.

I made my introductory remarks, never once at a loss for words. I knew my name, my purpose, and from the moment I began talking, I felt as if I were growing stronger and taller. I became a storyteller of the past summer, well, actually of the past several years, sharing openly and candidly the series of defining moments that had shaped my life. I could hear my voice echoing through the room. I was using words like *hope* and *promise*, all the while having a series of lightbulb moments, personal revelations about my own disappearance, and the treacherous journey that had nearly taken me down. It hit me suddenly that I had made a safe reentry to Planet Earth, and the experience had been transformational. I was not the same person I was five years ago. I was better. More resilient. Maybe even more whole. I can't explain why or how. I just was.

My body parts were suddenly reattached, reassembled. Today everything was working in sync.

My audience knew they were listening to someone who had traveled far to deliver this message—one that reeked of honesty and resolve. I could see in their eyes it was a message many of them were desperate to hear. We are living in an era of dire hopelessness; people are losing jobs, parents, friends, faith. We are surrounded by death. But I was standing in front of them, showing them it is possible to look death straight in the eye and not be engulfed by its power. On this day I felt like Superman.

"The children we serve are counting on us to show up," I said. My finger started pointing to people around the room. "You represent love. You are understanding. You are forgiveness. You, my friends, are their everything. Let's get busy."

I was talking slowly. Deliberately. Pausing between sentences. Knowing now that my audience was filling in their own narratives. Seeing the faces of their own students, maybe even their own children, all kids who need them. Some of their faces looked my way as if to acknowledge that one of those kids who had been let down was Alex. I can't remember precisely what I said, but I needed to assure them this was not a moment for sympathy. I reminded them none of us is exempt from loss. We must all be merchants of hope. I could see a look in some of their eyes, wondering how I could say this after losing my child.

I didn't have enough time to explain the nature and extent of my travels, but it didn't matter now. What mattered most was my own realization, in that precise instant, that I was at last comfortable in my own skin. I had come home.

December 31, 2009

Armen,

Hearing your exuberance about the trip is the biggest gift. It fills me with hope, relief, some sense of something I can't put my finger on. Hope because I never really think, even in my highest moments, that I'll be able to be really happy again, to have anything but a deep sadness encompassing my heart. It shows me that you can say yes to life once more. As you board the plane, you take us all with you. You are showing me that we can travel back and forth between Griefland and other places. Armen, maybe it's not a one-way journey after all.

Nancy

Lessons from Our Travels

January 1, 2010

Nancy,

Years from now we will be old women. I can see us in my mind's eye, rocking rhythmically in our chairs, a Mona Lisa smile on our faces, looking back and perhaps reminiscing on our many travels throughout the years. Occasionally we will read out loud from this book we are writing now, and one of us will stop the other and say, "Did you really say that?" And the other will say, "Yes, don't you remember—we were both unraveling that day . . ." I see us sitting under the warmth of Rachel's afghan, with each stitch reminding us of each step we've taken together.

More than anything I want to convey to you this morning that life has never been sweeter, richer, or fuller for me. I feel as if my toes are sinking into plush green grass. The sky is blue, there are flowers blooming, and the tranquil sound of water moving is music to the ear. Dare I say that the hole in my heart feels as if it is shrinking in size? Is that possible? Even if it should be temporary and short-lived, I feel more human and alive than I have felt in years . . .

Armen

Often, throughout this journey, I have found myself sitting at the dinner table with my husband or in a corner booth of my favorite watering hole with Nancy when the questions creep up. Would we trade places with anyone? Would we erase these memories? Go back in time? Permanently delete the painful parts? Our eye contact during these talks is intense, unwavering, focused.

A year ago Nancy and I barely knew each other, and today we are venturing to the most private parts of our inner worlds. We carefully construct questions, both of us probing beneath the surface, wondering if at some point one of us might answer yes, confessing she would gladly reverse roles, switch places, trade spots with those who have never endured this degree of loss. We stop ourselves short from what others might consider a mother's natural instinct to want her child back. Our bodies lean forward, fingers pressing firmly onto the paper that holds our written confessions. We whisper a forbidden commentary, the same banter we have e-mailed in the dark of the night, an unending debate that always ends with a simple "no." We can't go back. We are here now. This is our new place. Committing to paper our individual capacity to survive this place, we have compared notes often, regularly. We examine the writing as proof our hearts still beat, our blood still flows, our minds are still agile, our children are still with us through the myriad memories, photos, and sacred stories we have carefully resurrected onto these pages. Alex and Rachel started us on this journey, and it is at this juncture of our travels, at this precise destination point, that we fulfill a promise to them. And to ourselves.

On more than one occasion we have imagined they might reside here forever. These pages represent the only place on

Earth where they are safe and permanent. A fitting resting place, we say to ourselves. Sometimes we laugh. Sometimes the words drown in the salty residue of tears. We are learning to be comfortable with a new range of unpredictable emotions, more at ease now with ambiguity, with the idea of not knowing anything for certain. Rather than feel frightened, we have embraced the unknown, allowing it to unfold on its own terms. And if it never unfolds, we can accept the mystery as it is. Nancy and I agree that this new perspective is liberating. No one knows what to expect from us anymore. We have granted ourselves full permission to acknowledge and celebrate the many ways in which this new rhythm surprises us with each new day. Few friends can admit such freedom.

We have come to believe there can be something divine, a sort of knowledge and power that has occurred with death and grief. To travel this path, to remain standing for the duration of such an extraordinary journey, is a feat of significant proportions. We are stronger than ever now. The journey has been intense, hideous, terrifying, illuminating, fantastic. We have taken the worst event of our lives and made it the catalyst for the greatest work we will ever do. Death, in its devastation, has forced us to re-create ourselves. This rediscovery period is a passport to experience the world through a new lens. We have accepted the invitation.

We quiz ourselves often, wondering if it is possible to make this transformation without some unusual assistance—gifts, we call them, left behind by our children. We began looking for their stash—generous offerings of hidden knowledge that we hoped would be ours for the taking. After all, we were their moms.

One afternoon, while working on the final compilation of essays for this book, we met at our favorite restaurant. While hungry and thirsty patrons seated in the booths surrounding us complained about the heat, food portions, and broken presidential promises, we pulled and extracted words from the vital organs, connective tissue, and surrounding arteries and veins of ourselves.

We began a list. It would be something we could share with friends, family, readers, and visitors to Griefland. We wanted to show that one could emerge better than when one entered, strengthened by such a passage. We were fearful that without a list and evidence, no one would believe our outrageous claims—that we had weathered this unbelievable odyssey. We share with you our list.

The gift of bewilderment—We have learned to explore outside the margins of everyday life, to meander, poke around, allowing ourselves to meet life at all levels, from the ground up, reaching those places we once thought unattainable. We are becoming reacquainted with our imaginations, learning to remove the filters that often shield us from experiencing true joy. We have grown comfortable with not knowing, with celebrating the uncertainty of life.

The gift of vision—Death has taught us to look at people and situations differently. There is greater clarity. We can look beyond the obvious, seeing past things that, in the scheme of life, no longer matter. In a strange way, we have taken off our glasses in order to improve our eyesight. This new clarity of vision exists in fuzziness and ambiguity. We no longer expect to see easy explanations or the kind of simple answers that can camouflage what's really there.

The gift of compassion—Chance meetings, unusual circumstances, and unlikely friendships have sprouted up from everywhere. Death has opened a door or window for our humanity to escape and flourish, as well as to allow us to be on the receiving end of abundance and generosity.

The gift of priority—We have learned to say no to unwelcome requests, to invitations that might reduce us to small talk, to social obligations that we never liked in the first place. We have learned the art of saying, "No, thank you." No excuse required.

The gift of coming to your senses—After months of feeling compromised and consumed by the side effects of grief, we learned to tap other senses in order to appear functional. Our senses are sharpened, acute, on high alert to the world around us. Like cats, we can feel tremors and quakes before they occur; like songbirds, we can hear music playing off in the distance. This gift allows us to truly appreciate the smells and tastes of life, the sights and sounds of the world.

The gift of time travel—Minutes, hours, and days are distorted with death. At first, time freezes, causing a paralysis, stopping us in our tracks. We have learned to adjust the pace to serve our own needs. We can linger in time, find rest stops, prolong and extend a leisure-filled Saturday, while the world around us returns to its frenzied workweek without savoring a moment of the weekend. Staying present in a moment—whether it is sorrowful or joy-filled—is another lesson we have learned during our travels. It is not necessary or advisable to move in and out of our emotional states in a hurry to move on, move forward, move ahead. We discovered new layers of life hidden beneath our breakdowns and breakthrough moments.

The gift of patience—In the rush hour of life, we have taken solace in slowing down the heartbeat of everyday stressors, not making every deadline an emergency. We have taken care of loved ones, aging parents, grandchildren, husbands, within new borders now. We have redrawn boundaries between personal preservation and obligation. Without diminishing our love for these significant others, we have emerged from Griefland with a newfound sense of self-love, self-respect, and self-care. We are guardians of our own well-being. We recognize what we can reasonably do, what we cannot do, and we quietly acknowledge the space in between.

The gift of tolerance—Upon entering Griefland we learned immediately that there was no right or wrong way to grieve. We trust this might be true in many other aspects of life's trials. The best we can do in any given moment is the best we can do in any given moment. Period. We can now acknowledge where people are without trying to rescue, change, revive, or resuscitate them. We have grown content, comfortable with someone's decision to just be. We can sit down next to them, in silence, and let them know they are not alone. Relinquishing control has been one of Griefland's greatest lessons.

The gift of forgiveness—In posing the hard questions surrounding our children's deaths, we have realized that in order to forgive them, we have had to first forgive ourselves. In doing this, we also forgive those around us, anyone and everyone who touched the lives of our children, or might have influenced their actions. The act of forgiveness has allowed us to pull our feet from the quicksand of guilt and show others compassion.

The gift of resilience—Darwin once said that the species that was most likely to survive was not necessarily the most intelligent, but rather the species that was most adaptable, or able to change in an ever-changing environment. Griefland has made us resilient, able to adapt to a continuous stream of experiences, unpredictable weather patterns, lack of sleep, unusual apparitions, and fluctuating realities. We have learned to bend, as willows do, to each challenge, suspending disbelief long enough to see, to feel, to pass through, to morph.

The gift of memory—Grief has required us to exercise the muscle of memory. We have become storytellers, memory keepers, rediscovering buried treasures from the past. We excavate these precious memories from our children's infant years and school days, rekindling keepsake conversations between Rachel and Nancy, Alex and Armen. We replay and recite them out loud, varying the volume—we play them sometimes loud enough for the entire world to hear and other times softly, for our own ears in the form of a gentle lullaby or fairy tale. We have promised to pass these stories down to our grandchildren, preserving the memory, love, and legacy that remain.

The gift of vulnerability—We have become more human during the course of our travels, coming to a realization that grief removes a layer of parchment, a protective shield that now welcomes new emotions and feelings. We have also learned that grief cannot be tamed or controlled, nor should it be. Pain, sorrow, and hurt are part of the human condition; each adds texture and new meaning to life.

The gift of purpose—We have gone from feeling incompetent, inept, powerless, and hopeless to feeling brave and more sure of our purpose. We have recognized that it has been only through fully embracing our losses that we have found our ultimate purpose. Writing this book has brought us to the epicenter of love, generosity, acceptance, and bonding through the writing itself. Our deliverance has been twofold: We have been delivered from Griefland, as well as being able to deliver this book to you, our readers, some of whom have come so far in your own journeys through loss.

The gift of gratitude —We are still learning to look beyond our losses and see all that remains. We marvel at the sun and moon, starlit nights, a passing butterfly, or the sudden downpour of a summer rain. The sun faithfully returns to shine; life presses forward, and we can acknowledge openly and freely that we will always miss Alex and Rachel.

The gift of guidance and navigation—We have learned that sometimes in life you must get lost in order to find your way. Divergent paths lead us to uncomfortable places where traditional navigational guides, road maps, and instruments are utterly useless. We must rely instead on our keenest of senses, our intuition, and trust that the ground will not give way to our fears and the unknown.

The gift of silence—In a culture that values discourse, we have learned that the dialect of silence is priceless, allowing us to conduct the internal dialogue of reflection, introspection, the gathering of our own wits, which leads often to communication with our deeper selves, with our souls. In doing so, we can listen for the sounds that rise up from within.

The gift of true friendship—This, we have come to realize, is the ultimate gift of our tandem grief journeys. Our personal suitcases have exploded wide open, exposing the most intimate collection of thoughts and emotions, strengths and weaknesses, attributes and flaws, insecurities and confidences. We have carried each other across turbulent waters, we have held hands through jagged and steep terrain, and at the end of the day finally rested against each other's shoulders. The power of this journey has been in knowing that neither of us would abandon the other under even the most unthinkable of circumstances. As life moves forward, certain to bring new challenges to each of us, we know with great certainty that this friendship will never fail in rising to the occasion, and that we will always show up for each other.

The gift of risking everything for love—We have learned that beyond the pain of loss there is a beauty and splendor in risking everything for love. Many people live a lifetime without ever feeling the extraordinary potential for connection that lies within humans—to sacrifice and surrender themselves all for the sake and in the name of love. Parent to child, husband to wife, friend to friend—love trumps anything and everything.

Armen,

The first thing I see when I close my eyes and think of us as old women are two chairs, side by side, pointed in the same direction, a small table in between, a bottle of Cabernet between us, two colored crystal glasses. I see us in the spring, in a garden full of purple forget-me-nots, a carpet of grass under our feet. I shall read poetry and short stories to you, and you will sip your wine, and when my eyes grow tired, you will read aloud to me, and I shall sip mine. And the memories we will share about our travels through Griefland will be like precious rubies, gems that will remind us of our fortitude and passion, our need for friends. Good friends.

Nancy

Armen's Acknowledgments

Through thick and thin, for better or worse, Dan, you have remained the one constant in this turbulent, upside-down journey. As book writing took over my days and nights, the only promise you made me keep was to tell the whole truth and nothing but the truth. You gave me time, space, and permission to grieve out loud. I love you beyond words.

Danielle, I cannot imagine what it feels like to lose a sibling. While both of us lost Alex, each of us navigated this journey in her own unique way. Amid your sadness, you found courage to believe in life and love, blessing our family with two beautiful granddaughters and a set of amazing twins. In looking into their eyes, I see an infinite universe abundant with hope.

Jessica, you were the true love of Alex's life. Together, you brought Logan into this world. He is a magical child, with a mind and future all his own. And you are a loving and exceptional parent. Take good care of our "angel boy."

To Anne Murphy, my friend and colleague. I will never forget the day you wrote me about Nancy. Your generosity of spirit and heartfelt gesture to help a friend changed my life. Thank you, dear heart.

To the extraordinary women of the Cemetery Club: Each of you has a special story, a hole that sears your heart, but enormous will to keep standing. This book is a tribute to your strength, stamina, and spirit.

To Robert Setrakian, for igniting my writing passion and resuscitating my love for William Saroyan, whose famous words, "In the time of your life, live," are forever etched in my heart.

To Doug Rice, my writing professor and confidant, who implored me to dig deep to excavate the stories and memories that mattered most. Your lectures were my oxygen. Without you and Summer Arts, I would still be crafting chapter 1.

Our first-draft manuscript readers were the first to believe in us. To Paul Chaderjian, Cynthia Karraker, Terri Connell, Jennifer Quinn-Yovino, Anne Murphy—thank you for accompanying us to Griefland, not knowing what the journey might entail.

To Zov Karamardian, for introducing us to Christine Schwab, our first editor, whose willingness to ask the tough questions guided us through the dark and treacherous crevices of our personal stories.

To my mother Virginia Derian, sisters Alyce Berard and Edie Bieber, niece Lauren Haskell, and friends Gail Perry Henricksen, Jeanne Parnagian, Sarabeth Rothfeld, Carol Rau, Cynthia Karraker, Beth Marney Emerian, Chris Young, Carolyn Golden, Peggy Stathem, and Jennifer Quinn-Yovino—thank you for embracing both my breakdowns and breakthroughs. You are the true wonder women in my life.

To Romain Pacaud, the lost French boy who found me at the Charles de Gaulle Airport in Paris on the one-year anniversary of Alex's death. *Je t'embrasse toujours.* Maybe someday we will translate this book into French.

These acknowledgments would not be complete without a note of thanks to our fictitious waiter at the Griefland Cafe. As he evolved through our imaginative descriptions, we fell head over heels for his intuitive powers, his quiet and discreet treatment of us, especially on those days when we were teetering and off balance.

"Au Clair de la Lune" is a score of music I learned as a child and have loved my entire life. Meeting Claire Gerus, our agent, opened up the heavens and brought stars to our doorstep. Thank you, Claire, for giving us the moon so eloquently wrapped in your expertise and know-how.

To Lara Asher and Globe Pequot Press, for being a perfect fit for the final leg of this extraordinary journey. From our very first communiqué, your enthusiasm and commitment to this project, and to us, was assurance of a safe landing.

For Alex, my boy who wanted to fly. Although I originally envisioned you living in narrative form on these pages, I have come to realize that those imaginary wings now transport you to destinations that exceed all of our wildest dreams. Whether you are close by or in flight, I love you, Superman.

And finally, to Nancy, my writing partner. We had no idea where we were headed when we first met and decided to cross the borders of Griefland in tandem. You are an amazing woman, a woman of substance, a forever friend and sister. I look forward to many more words between us in the coming years.

Nancy's Acknowledgments

First, to Anne Murphy, the woman who introduced me to Armen, and the catalyst for this magical alliance. To our agent Claire Gerus, who possesses an indomitably wild and tenacious spirit that matches ours, and whose unrelenting efforts buoyed us in the darkest of times. You are a taskmaster, a treasure, a sister. Lara Asher, the visionary who took a chance on a couple of unknown writers—thank you for bringing this project to fruition, for believing in its power from the day you first read the manuscript.

To Mike Clifton, thank you for seeing what this was before we did, and for pushing me to the limits as you always have, and to Lillian Faderman, for seeming to drop everything time and again to ask important questions and provide encouragement, guidance, and faith.

My cousins, soul mates, and friends—Janice Trimble, Gerry Sarkisian, Arlene Cartozian, Pat Towne, Rosemary Andrew, Sharon Dobie, Maggie Webley, Terese Cenci McGee, Michelle Chun-Leroy, Shareen Grogan, and Jane Blood-Siegfried—who have been alongside me every inch of this journey, thank you for providing everything from encouragement, love, and support to feedback on the early manuscript. To Christine Schwab and Bonnie Hearn Hill, for your early edits and guidance, and undaunted faith.

To my parents-in-law, Sally and Mac Miller, who have fed and sheltered me, listened to my rants and cries, and loved me through the worst of times. To Aunt Neva Hofemann, the godsend who gave me the laptop that ended up being my lifeline and tool to write this book. To Karen Miller, my sister-in-law, who has been supportive and nurturing during what has been the hardest part of my life. To my special auntie, Carol Shimmon, my main role model. You show me every day that it is possible to lose a child—even two now—and still find joy in life, even amid the tears.

Thanks to my personal computer guru, Constance Chang, who seems to be on call for every technical meltdown I have had in the last nearly twenty years, and especially during the writing of this book.

To Norm Thibault and Garth Lasater, Rachel's therapists at Cross Creek School in Utah, for all the hours you spent trying to save her, and the unconditional love you showed to her, which she felt. Always know that. Thanks to my beautiful niece, Jenny Weiner, nephew Stephan Weiner, Cortney Holmes, and Rory Hejtmanek, her best friends, among many others, who miss her beyond description.

To my children Joshua and Jessica, who navigate their own grief journeys while carving out the paths of their lives without their sister. She knew you loved her; never doubt that.

Rachel, my cubby. What a strange gift you have given me. I am beyond grateful for the time we had, the tremendous impact you have made on my life, and on the lives of everyone who knew you. Our last hug—the longest one we ever had—is emblazoned on my heart; I will feel it all the days of my life.

Most of all, Randy. You took care of my every need during all the days and nights I was obsessed with writing. Thank you for creating the most beautiful garden in the world for me, a retreat and haven that even Monet would envy. For cooking, cleaning, picking me up off the floor time and again. Every word has been for you.

Armen, my love, my suitcase is already packed. Give me a minute to get over the jet lag—then we can decide where we're going next.

About the Authors

Armen Bacon is a wife, mother, grandmother, professional woman, and author. A passion for people, travel, and writing—these are the things that run through her veins. She is a story-teller. A memory keeper. A writer of docu-memories for the soul and the human condition, "connective tissue that makes us all more human," she says. For two decades, Armen has served as Administrator of Communications & Public Relations for the Fresno County Office of Education. She is also a regular contributor to the *Fresno Bee* and since 2006 has written/voiced a daily radio feature titled *Live, Laugh, Love* for KJWL 99.3. Armen holds a bachelor's degree in psychology from California State University, Fresno, and a master's degree in organizational management. She is a four-year artisan alum from the CSU Summer Arts Program where she studied memoir, poetic prose, narrative nonfiction, and flash fiction. She resides in Fresno, California, with her husband, Dan, and draws inspiration from family, friends, and her five grandchildren: Logan, Arden, Ani, and twins, Dennis and Sosi. Her collection of *Fresno Bee* columns is slated for publication soon, titled, *My Name Is Armen, A Life in Column Inches.* Write to Armen at armen@griefland.com.

Nancy Miller is a wife and mother, composition instructor and writer. She has mentored students at the university and junior college levels for more than seventeen years and worked as managing editor and staff writer for *The Business Journal* and Pacific Publishing Group in Fresno for more than six. She was instrumental in creating a writing center at Fresno High School and at Fresno City College and has been a senior writing consultant for National University's Online Writing Centers for more than a decade. Working with troubled teenagers and their families, she has led several support groups locally and has assisted in staffing seminars for parents who made the difficult decision of admitting their at-risk teenagers to rehabilitative schools located across the nation. She continues supporting families who have lost children to drug abuse. She received her master's degree in English literature from California State University, Fresno, and makes her debut in the powerful memoir, *Griefland,* co-authored with Armen Bacon. She has recently moved to Olympia, Washington, with her husband, Randy, and their Rhodesian ridgeback, Elsa, and is currently working on a second anthology of essays. Write to Nancy at nancy@griefland.com.